LEADERSHIP
EDUCATION
in
the
LOCAL
CHURCH

LEADERSHIP
EDUCATION
in
the
LOCAL
CHURCH

by

Price H. Gwynn, Jr.

Published for the
COOPERATIVE PUBLISHING ASSOCIATION
by
THE WESTMINSTER PRESS
Philadelphia

PRINTED IN THE UNITED STATES OF AMERICA

CONTENTS

Chapter I

BASIC PRINCIPLES

"Whom Shall I Send, and Who Will Go for Us?"

God's call for leaders to convey the truth of his Word is as urgent today as it was in the time of Isaiah. Never before were there so many opportunities for useful service in the work of the Church. Never was there greater need for teaching the gospel of our Lord and Saviour, Jesus Christ. Response to this challenge during the next few years may determine the destiny of the Protestant faith. A free Church can endure only if devoted men and women gladly volunteer for its educational task. They can successfully transmit the religion they believe only if they are adequately prepared for the responsibility they have assumed.

Who Can Estimate the Worth of a Faithful Christian Teacher?

Let us reply with chapters from the lives of two great Americans.

The matron of an orphan asylum in Washington, D. C., used a horsewhip on little Jimmy West and put him on a bread-and-water diet. She said he was evading his chores by pretending to be sick. Fortunately a friend of Jimmy's mother recalled a promise to the dying woman and went to call on the unhappy youngster. She insisted on taking the boy to a doctor and it was discovered that he had a tubercular hip.

For over a year he lay strapped to a board. The doctors agreed that his case was hopeless. Since the hospital could do nothing further for him, the orphanage was asked to send for the child. The matron refused to do so. How could she take care of a helpless cripple? The hospital superintendent finally called a cab and gave careful instructions to the driver. In the gathering darkness he drove up to the orphan asylum, deposited the boy and his crutches inside the door, and hurried away. Jimmy was found there by an older girl when she locked up for the night. What chance was there for this unwanted eight-year-old child? None at all, according to accepted ideas of social workers and psychologists. He seemed doomed, if he lived at all, to grow up crippled in both body and soul.

Then a miracle! A Sunday school was held regularly at the orphanage and Jimmy's class was taught by the man in charge of the heating plant. He was a laboring man, but he had deep Christian convictions which he shared with the boy. Jimmy came to believe God had a purpose for him. In later years he said: " I began to feel the first throb of spiritual emotion. With this came the feeling that God did not expect me or any human being to remain hopeless human wreckage. The faith that I acquired in God during my youth gave me strength, ambition, and determination above all other things when my life seemed so hopelessly futile."

From this point on the career of James E. West reads like a fairy tale in which anything can happen. He put himself through school and became a lawyer, but his main interest was always in underprivileged children. Through his work for the children of Washington, he came to the attention of President Theodore Roosevelt. When the Boy Scouts of America was chartered by Congress, Mr. West was asked to become the chief executive.

Due to the influence of his Sunday school training, the law that " A Boy Scout is reverent " was made the climax of the American Scout code, although it was not included in the original standards of the British organization. "Because of my own personal experience," said Mr. West, " I was insistent on one point, that we emphasize religion in the life of the boy."

A Sunday school teacher brought hope to a hopeless child through the power of religious faith, and millions of Boy Scouts have developed a finer sense of reverence and of duty to God because of the inspiration that he gave to James E. West.[1]

One of the greatest pulpit orators ever produced in this country

[1] From a collection of stories gathered by Dr. Walter D. Cavert, 430 University Building, 120 E. Washington Street, Syracuse 2, New York.

is reported to have been led to Christ and influenced to enter the
gospel ministry by a humble Sunday school teacher in the moun-
tains of western North Carolina.

These two stories could be multiplied by a thousand to show
that God alone can estimate the worth of a faithful Christian
teacher.

Nevertheless, Protestant churches face a serious problem in
their dependence upon a volunteer leadership for the major responsibility in transmitting the Christian heritage. The Roman
Catholic Church has trained its teaching orders to be used in the
achievement of this task. But Protestants must add to their professional leadership a host of willing workers who can give only
their spare time to the cause of Christian education.

What Do We Mean by Leadership Education?

Leadership education is the process of finding and training
workers in the Church, who will be able to do at least these two
things:

1. Transmit the Christian heritage: (a) by formal teaching of
the gospel; (b) by example of their lives — demonstration of un-
swerving loyalty to Jesus Christ; (c) by joint experimentation in
Christian living.

2. Bring others to Christ — that is, into: (a) a saving fellowship
or relationship with Jesus Christ — redemption of the human
spirit; (b) commitment of the whole life to the service of the
Master — discipleship.

The content of leadership education is to be found in a study
of human behavior, a thorough knowledge and understanding of
the Christian message, and gradual mastery of the most successful
methods to be used in directing the teaching-learning process.
The first supplies the psychological information about human
beings, which leads to an easy and natural approach in dealing
with their spiritual needs. The second refers to the source materials in which the truth of our revealed religion is found, primarily, the Bible and the history of the Christian Church. The third
comprehends the technique involved in making a vital interpretation of the truth.

Recruiting deeply spiritual men and women for the teaching task of the Church and making possible for them a program of preparation in order to do the job effectively — in this combination we have the primary function of leadership education.

What Are Desirable Traits in a Christian Leader?

Dr. Forrest L. Knapp has given us a sample of Christian leadership in the dedication of his book *Leadership Education in the Church.* It reads as follows:

To My Mother and Father
OLIVE R. AND MELVIN S. KNAPP
Who Began During My Early Years to Demonstrate Leadership by Expecting Me to Assume Responsibility According to My Capacity, Encouraging Me to Use Initiative in Meeting My Problems, Permitting Reasonable Freedom of Choice and of Experimentation, Helping Me to Achieve Success in Significant Enterprises, Insisting Upon Integrity and Dependability in All Things, and by Exemplifying Christian Character

Three things stand out in this description of faithful parents, who led their son into the loyal service of the Master. One is the power to realize the capacity and initiative in others. A second is the insistent demand that the one being guided shall live up to the best that is in him. And the third is ability to share in everyday living the high ideals and purposes of the Christian religion.

Many lists have been made of the qualifications that should be found in the teacher of the Protestant faith. The following would appear to be basic.

1. A deep and abiding Christian experience.
2. A persistent longing to share that experience with others.
3. A sure knowledge of what the Bible teaches.
4. A fair understanding of how personality develops.
5. Training in the best educational practice afforded by the example and experimentation of those most successful in the field.

Perhaps we can personalize the ideal for which we are striving by a description of the effective teacher or leader in Christian service.

George Herbert Palmer was probably the most dearly beloved teacher Harvard ever had. Once upon a time he wrote a brief essay which he entitled "The Ideal Teacher." That little monograph should be required reading for every person charged with the instruction of youth. Palmer, out of his long years of rich experience, advanced four characteristics of the successful teacher.

First of all, the vital teacher must have an aptitude for unselfish sharing. He should be able, by the power of the imagination, to put himself in the pupil's place and understand with sympathy the difficulties that beset his progress. This capacity to sense the need of others should become habitual and instinctive — a matter of intuitive insight on the part of the teacher. It enables him to give the best that he has to his disciple, and so to kindle in his heart a passion for learning. The second qualification is an accumulated wealth of knowledge. The growing teacher gathers a great storehouse of material and suggestion, which he can use in helping the student to satisfy his curiosity. He is equipped to nourish the expanding intellectual life of those committed to his care. Even to teach a small thing well, one must have a large knowledge of it. Palmer in this connection makes use of a very striking phrase. He says that one cannot constantly teach up to the edge of his knowledge without someday falling off. Persistent exploration in fresh fields of information is required to avoid stagnation and monotony. A third quality of the good teacher is the ability to invigorate life through knowledge. This involves a vital transmission that relieves the drudgery of piecemeal learning. Knowledge is power only as it is appropriated by the student and used to feed his hungry soul. The accumulation of facts should lead to critical and constructive action. Facts, says Dr. Palmer, are pernicious when they enslave or fail to quicken the mind that grasps them. Teaching should unfold pupil and teacher together. Finally, the true teacher must have a readiness to be forgotten. His purpose is not to advertise himself, but to display the truth and make it winsome. For those of us who teach religion this means that Christ occupies the center of the stage, and the learner falls in love with him rather than with his instructor.

Dr. Palmer, in his brief description of the ideal teacher, issues a mighty challenge to all of us who have assumed the responsibility of guiding other lives. The standards he sets, though they may seem to be beyond our reach, are none too high. Effective teaching involves the hardest kind of work — frequently, indeed, bitter discouragement, because the results obtained fall so far short of the potentialities revealed. The teacher is the key to all educational progress. Handsome buildings conveniently arranged are a great asset. Modern equipment multiplies the usefulness of the good teacher. But the central factor in developing the life of the boy or girl is the person who brings to bear upon him the impact of his character and enthusiasm. Every one of us, as we survey the years, pays silent tribute to some great teacher who opened up the vistas of knowledge and set us on fire with a desire to explore their farthest reaches. Therefore, with Dr. Palmer's ideal teacher as a touchstone, let us go farther in exposing the qualities of successful teaching.

The teacher is a guide — an opener of doors, a blazer of trails, a revealer of pitfalls and dangers. When the ocean liner arrives at the entrance to New York harbor, it drops anchor and waits for the arrival of a dumpy little tug, which brings the harbor pilot. Under his skillful guidance the great ship is brought safely to dock. This concept of the teacher as a guide is rich in possibilities for growth on the part of both learner and master. Two of its implications are worthy of careful study.

A guide must be trustworthy. He is one who knows the way and has traveled it many times before. He should be thoroughly familiar with every turn in the road. His knowledge of the ground to be covered must be recent and comprehensive. Memory, unless refreshed, fades into uncertainty. New hazards appear in the trail with the passage of the years. For the teacher in the church school this means a deep and abiding religious experience. It implies the constant replenishment of personal faith by a regular program of Bible study and prayer. It puts upon the teacher the obligation to keep abreast of the peculiar difficulties and temptations that accompany a rapidly changing social order. An example above reproach is a minimal essential. And thorough preparation of every lesson follows as a logical conclusion of the whole matter.

More important still is the urgent demand that the motives of the guide shall be beyond question. Devotion to the interests of his pupils should be the driving power in the life of every Sunday school teacher. Let those who are teaching only out of a sense of duty resign their positions at once. Others who are working primarily for the praise of men should resolve the conflict between self-interest and service before they continue with their sacred task. Men and women who are not wholly surrendered to the will of God will lead their pupils astray.

The function of the true guide is leadership rather than dictation. He must not only know the way, but he must inspire confidence and co-operation in those for whose safe conduct he has assumed responsibility. The courage of his followers may wane, but his should never falter. When their strength declines because the road seems hard and difficult, his faith and enthusiasm should carry them on to the next objective. He is ever the incarnation of self-discipline and unfailing devotion. So the teacher of religion must have patience and understanding and a willingness to be consumed in the success and failure of his students. A discriminating knowledge of human need is his greatest asset.

The successful teacher is an interpreter. Life is full of contradiction, frustration, and disappointment. A thoughtful young mind, observing the insane behavior of whole nations today, wonders if there is any plan or purpose in the universe. Why does God permit half the world to go mad and repudiate every principle of decent morality? In the midst of the prevailing confusion, the teacher of the Christian religion interprets God's will. He makes clear the manifestation of God's love. He offers a philosophy of life that brings meaning and significance into human experience.

Two gifts are prerequisite to fruitful interpretation. One is the gift of insight. Only the pure in heart are blessed with religious insight. Only those who make their belief a practical, working order of applied Christianity can grasp the purposes of God. Laborious study multiplies the chances of enlightenment. Without faith that issues in obedience it is impossible to please Him. The other tool of interpretation is the power of articulation. A teacher who gets beneath the surface of formal instruction is able to translate his insights into vivid, homely language. He brings home the truth he has appropriated by illustration, by picture, by symbol, and by living demonstration of its control in his own conduct. It is not necessary that he be eloquent in words. But his explanation must be clear, simple, sincere, and practical. If his interpretation of the gospel is valid, it meets the pressing problems of pupils who face the perplexities of a new and different day.

How great is our need for interpreters in this age of doubt and fear! We shall never lack for the scholar in religion — the man who by faithful research increases our knowledge of Christ and his mission. But good interpreters are scarce. Progress is measured by the ability of teachers to translate the findings of the investigator into the language of the common people. The message of the gospel remains the same from generation to generation. But a fresh and life-giving application of its eternal principles is required by each changing cycle of human experience.

The effective teacher is always a discoverer. He looks at the boy or girl who seeks his guidance with an air of eager expectancy. With reverence he estimates the limitless possibilities of every pupil who comes inside the orbit of his influence. Humbled and fascinated, he becomes a co-worker with God in the unfolding of personality. His is the duty and the privilege of revealing to the learner his true talents. Because he knows his pupil he finds within him potentialities that go unnoticed by others. Thomas Aquinas came up from southern Italy for the study of theology at the University of Paris. He was so clumsy and backward socially that his classmates called him " the dumb ox from Sicily." So great was his embarrassment in the midst of strange surroundings that he would fain have returned to his plow. But his teacher, Albertus Magnus, discerned beneath the rough exterior of the country boy a spark of divine genius. He gave him every encouragement and full opportunity to prove his worth. Out of that fellowship came the great theologian of the Roman Catholic Church and one of the sublimest thinkers of all time.

Think of Helen Keller's teacher — faced by insurmountable obstacles as she labored to pierce through the wall of darkness that separated her pupil from the outside world. Surely she would have been forgiven if she had despaired of her job. But she believed she had discovered in the little girl the power of response, if she could only find the key to the avenue of communication. She and her pupil must have gone through hours of agonizing struggle as they sought a means of contact between mind and mind. The magnificent personality of Helen Keller as we know her today is ample testimony to her teacher's faith.

The creative teacher is always finding opportunities for the self-realization of his students. Here is a child who is sensitive and retiring. Because of timidity, he hesitates to reveal his heart. Through gentle love and skillful manipulation the teacher draws him out. He designs for the boy a place of usefulness in the life of the group, and thus promotes in his mind a feeling of confidence and success. Here is another child who is bold and irreverent. Multiplied chances for activity under the positive control of Christian discipline curb his reckless spirit and turn his energies into channels of noble service. The greatest tribute that can come to a teacher is the remark of his pupil: " I never knew what was in me until I met Mr. A."

The conscientious teacher is ever a learner. He girds his mind from day to day by fresh explorations in the great storehouse of truth. Those who dare to teach should know both their facts and their pupils. They must constantly enrich their understanding of human nature. The Bible is the greatest textbook of psychology ever written. To its discerning wisdom the teacher of religion adds the most recent discoveries of trustworthy leaders in the study of human development. The ambitious teacher persistently seeks for new methods of presenting the Master's message. He remembers the wide range of individual differences in his pupils and carefully prepares a variety of approaches so as to catch and hold the attention of them all. The teacher who discounts the value of method is like the carpenter who allows his saw or his plane to become dull. The only difference is that we discharge the carpenter, while all too frequently we retain the services of the negligent teacher. He who would impart spiritual truth must work under the perpetual guidance of the Holy Spirit. He must be willing to learn in the school of God's discipline. The discoverer of God's will grows in grace from day to day. His teaching is progressively invigorated by the steady renewal of his spiritual life.

We need to remind ourselves that Jesus was the Master Teacher. In the record of the Gospels we find infinite resources for improvement of the teaching art. Jesus understood human beings. He had a message for all classes because he spoke their language. He always appealed to the deepest desires of the human heart. The Master was never satisfied with less than the best from his disciples. With infinite patience he strengthened the will of those who failed. Through homely illustrations and abundant life situations he helped his pupils to apply the doctrines that he taught. We cannot live the life that Jesus lived. But as teachers of his gospel we do well to emulate his example and follow in his footsteps.

What Should Be Our Aims in Leadership Education?

" The Purpose of Christian Leadership Education " is the title of a statement recently approved by the Committee on Leadership Education of the Division of Christian Education, National Council of the Churches of Christ in the United States of America. The following summary of goals is influenced by the work and findings of that Committee.

Christian leadership education seeks to nurture growing persons in the Christian life, to strengthen their faith and their knowledge of the will of God and of the mind of Christ. It seeks to help them to make their attitudes, appreciations, hopes, purposes, and loyalties thoroughly Christian, and to develop ways of sharing this knowledge and experience and faith with other growing persons.

1. Persons learn through experience. Leadership for the Church is developed both through courses and conferences and through continued guided experiences in training which are integral to the ongoing work of the Church.

2. God's revelation is basic to Christian teaching as well as the recorded experiences of others who have come in contact with

his power and grace. Hence, each worker in the Church should be led to a careful and reverent study of the Bible and other religious literature.

3. We learn through association with other persons. Therefore, all leaders should share in group experiences of worship, service, planning, and training.

4. Inner drive or motivation is essential for success in any venture. We are also stimulated by appreciation from the group of which we are a part. Therefore, a person should be encouraged to accept tasks that seem to be suited to his abilities, and he should be given the guidance, training, and recognition that will lead him to success in his work.

5. Most important of all in guiding others are the attitudes and personality of the teacher or leader. Hence, a major objective of leadership education is the personal enrichment of the lives of all Church workers.

A virile Protestant faith calls for intelligence and understanding. One of its basic assumptions is that those who embrace its teachings will be able to read and interpret the Bible for themselves. The achievement of this goal demands a trained leadership worthy of confidence and equipped to guide a liberated people. In producing the men and women we need for this task, a heavy responsibility rests upon the home, the Church, and the theological seminary. Family religion, through fellowship and example, sets early patterns for spiritual growth. The Church, through its various activities and Christian colleges, supplies the more formal aspects of leadership training. And upon the seminary falls the inescapable obligation of producing an educationally minded ministry. Without pastors who appreciate the educational function of the Church, there is little hope of perpetuating the great Protestant contribution and insight.

History reveals that freedom prevails wherever the message of the Reformation is adequately taught and faithfully exemplified. Despotism takes root whenever this message is neglected or falsely portrayed. Genuine democracy is possible only when built upon the great foundation stones of a free Christian religion. The

American way of life is undergirded by the sublime teachings of Jesus regarding the rights of man and his obligation to God and community. Armies and navies, even atomic energy, will fail to safeguard our liberties if we cease to transmit his precepts. Let our children forget that only God is " Lord of the conscience," that human rights supersede property rights, that every man is accountable for the deeds done in this life, that all human beings are God's creatures and his potential children — let the effective teaching of these supreme truths lapse — and chains for both body and soul begin to be forged.

The truth of the matter is that the program of Protestant Christian education in the United States suffers everywhere for the lack of trained leadership to carry the burden of its important mission. The pattern of religious education must meet the demands of the times. It must contain an element of vision, else the people perish. Without the prophetic touch in education the life of the nation becomes static and the outlook of the Church is turned upon the past rather than the future. The Protestant Churches must take up again the task in which they so nobly pioneered and recapture the faith of their founders in a thorough preparation of leaders for imparting the " good news."

The time has arrived in the history of the Church when the vision of the churchman and the statesman is demanded if we are to project an adequate program of education for leadership. No longer will antiquated methods of teaching and guidance serve to transmit the Christian heritage. Protestants can ill afford to be put to shame by the public schools, by industry, and even by the Government in discovering and preparing leaders to carry on the work of the Church. A free Church must educate or perish. Success in education depends upon a trained personnel to achieve positive commitment and growth in Christian character.

Chapter II

ORGANIZING AND PLANNING THE WORK

The system under which we work and the spirit that surrounds us make all the difference in the world. A child grows and prospers in an atmosphere of order, understanding, and appreciation. The firm that plans its work carefully, divides duties fairly, and gives appropriate recognition to devoted service has an advantage in finding and keeping good workers. So it is with the program of Christian nurture. The first step in leadership education is to create a situation in which those who are called to serve the Master are encouraged to give the best they have instead of being persistently ignored or frustrated.

There is nothing particularly difficult in achieving this goal. The essential thing is the will to do it. Successful organization and administration depend upon human relations rather than upon money, big buildings, and elaborate equipment. One poor Sunday school secretary can go a long way toward defeating the purpose of the entire church school. On the other hand, the earnest teacher with only a Bible and the literature furnished by her church can perform miracles, provided she has the intelligent support and co-operation of those in authority.

What Is the Function of the Minister?

Ultimate responsibility for the educational task of the church rests squarely upon the shoulders of the pastor. The Catholic Church succeeds in getting this across to the priesthood. But Protestant seminaries do not always make the obligation clear to their students. The minister is the spiritual leader of the congregation. The people respect and support the things upon which he puts emphasis. They are likely to neglect the interests to which he is indifferent. Because of his specialized training they look to him for guidance in all the activities of the church.

Some Things the Minister Can and Ought to Do as an Educational Statesman

1. See that the program of Christian education is organized and administered in accord with the discipline of the church.

2. Counsel with officers, teachers, and other workers concerning their problems, expressing appreciation for their fidelity, and encouraging them to undertake new ventures in their respective fields.

3. Attend as often as possible meetings of the body responsible for Christian education in the local church, as well as the meetings of the workers' conference.

4. Visit and observe classes in the church school — fulfill the function of a sympathetic supervisor.

5. Preach from time to time on the importance of Christian education in the home. The spiritual leadership of the pastor at this point is essential if any progress is to be made.

6. Call attention to significant developments in Christian education literature and ways of teaching.

7. Take a leading part in the annual service of recognition held in honor of the Christian education staff.

8. Help in discovering and enlisting new leaders.

9. Conduct a leadership training class occasionally — an experience which reveals the personal difficulties of those who are commissioned to transmit the Christian heritage in his church and reminds him of the hard work which must accompany effective teaching.

10. Emphasize the solemn obligation of parents for the religious nurture of their children and urge them to co-operate with the church school.

Some Things the Minister Should Not Do

1. Take over the general administration of the church school — serve as superintendent.

2. Teach a class regularly.

3. Try to dictate to the lay leaders, who have been chosen for these responsibilities.

4. The minister should not assume tasks in the program of Christian education, his assumption of which would encourage members of the church to become complacent or to shirk their duty. He should not deprive some potential lay leader of his legitimate opportunity. Furthermore, he is likely to depreciate his usefulness as a preacher when he loads himself with extra duties Sunday morning.

If the church is unfortunate enough to get a pastor whose interest in Christian education is slight or perfunctory, two things are in order: Prayer should be made by devout men and women for a change of heart. Then, with the background of this concern, officers of the church should counsel with him about their great opportunity and the need of his help.

It is almost universally true that an educationally minded minister has a growing church. His interest is a great factor in developing the lay leaders who are responsible for the program of Christian nurture and outreach.

How Does the Congregation Take Hold?

It would hardly seem necessary to emphasize the sharing process in any Christian enterprise. The democratic right to be heard and to make suggestion is basic in the gospel of Jesus. But the truth is that many church schools still exist where the counsel of those who carry the burden of instruction and guidance is seldom, if ever, sought. In many more the intention of general participation and support is present, but an understanding of how it can be achieved is lacking. Our people need training in effective methods of group discussion and action. Church school officers, teachers, counselors, and representative parents should all have a part in planning for Christian education in the local church. How this end can be secured without time-wasting argument will appear as we proceed.

Where Should Authority Be Centered?

If success is to be achieved in any co-operative endeavor, some one group must be granted the authority to make final decisions and determine long-range policies. Experience has shown that the most effective type of organization for this purpose in the local church is a committee, or board, of Christian education, chosen by the governing body of the congregation. This arrangement allows for representation of the various interests that make up the program of Christian education, and for inclusion of certain other able people, who perhaps have an unusual contribution to make to the educational progress of the church. The pastor and the director of religious education, if there is one, would always be ex officio members of the group. Specifically, what are its functions?

The Board of Christian Education in the Local Church

1. Designs the policies and plans the total program for all the educational work of the church. It undertakes to direct and supervise the various activities that contribute to this end, such as: Children's Work; Youth Programs; Adult Work; Christian Family Life; Weekday Religious Education; Musical Organizations; Camp and Conference Activities; Women's Work and Men's Work; Classes in Preparation for Church Membership; and Character Building Agencies Working in Co-operation with the Church — Boy Scouts, for example. This board also has the responsibility of seeing that Educational Evangelism, Leadership Education, Stewardship, Social Education and Action, Missionary Education, and similar emphases are given balanced consideration in each age group, and are integrated into the total educational program of the church.

2. Co-ordinates all the elements of the Christian education program, so as to avoid overlapping, neglect of important items, conflicting viewpoints and procedures, and mutual interference.

3. Provides the particular resource and teaching materials that will be used in the church.

4. Sets up a budget for the church school, which should be in-

corporated in the total budget of the church.

5. Surveys the educational needs of the entire church constituency and evaluates the present program in the light of those needs, suggesting from time to time desirable changes and ways of improvement.

6. Examines building, equipment, and furnishings, to discover whether they meet the requirements for successful educational activity, and makes recommendations for their adaptation or replacement.

7. Enlists and trains workers for the various positions of leadership.

8. Selects goals and makes plans for reaching them by a program of annual planning.

9. Seeks to develop an educational consciousness in the congregation and secure enthusiastic support from the church membership for a worthy program of Christian education.

10. Chooses representatives from its number to participate in community projects of a character-building nature and determines the extent of co-operation in such activities — athletic leagues, music festivals, Christmas celebrations, for example.

Who Should Be on the Board of Christian Education?

1. Always one or more members of the governing body or chief official board of the church.

2. Persons who have special interest in the work of Christian education and are able to give substantial portions of their time to its pursuit.

3. Persons who represent various groups or aspects of the total program through experience, training, and interest.

4. Persons temporarily prevented from active participation in the local program of Christian education, but with wide experience or special training in Church or educational work — for example, a specialist in public-school administration, who travels and is therefore prevented from taking a position in the church school.

How Large Should the Board Be?

It should be large enough to represent the major educational organizations in the program of Christian education and the best leadership in the church. However, its membership should be small enough to make frequent full meetings possible. In churches of 100–250 members, 5 to 7 should be sufficient. Larger churches may need 12 or more on the committee. Additional help may be co-opted at any time for special projects or service on specific subcommittees.

How Shall the Board Be Organized, and How Often Should It Meet?

The board should have a chairman who will take his job seriously — a person of imagination, initiative, and executive ability. It also needs a secretary to keep the records and to see that actions taken are reported promptly to the persons and groups involved. Much of the more significant work of the board will be done by it as a committee of the whole, since its responsibilities cover the entire educational program of the church. Especially is this true in the smaller church.

There will be times, however, when it will want to delegate certain specific duties to individuals or special subcommittees. In some churches it may be wise to have persons or standing subcommittees representing certain particular interests or groups and reporting regularly to the board. The following divisions of the total program might thus be assured of continued review and emphasis: Children's Work; Youth Programs; Adult Work; Social Education and Action; Leadership Education; Stewardship and Vocation; Missionary Education and Outreach.

The board will render a helpful service by appointing someone to make and keep on display a Program Calendar to avoid conflicts and to remind those involved of the items for which preparation should be made far in advance. Church work continually suffers from lack of proper advance planning.

Local needs will determine how often the board meets. Once a month may be desirable if the load is heavy. Certainly the group should convene at least once each quarter to discharge the important task committed to its care. Doubtless the work of the board can be expedited by sitting in from time to time on the meetings of the workers' conference.

Work of the Committee on Leadership Education

This committee is responsible for finding and training workers in the local church. In all cases it has a twofold function:

1. Discovery and enlistment of the people best qualified to take the lead in the church's program of Christian education.

2. Provision for keeping those thus commissioned in touch with fruitful opportunities for self-improvement.

Among its most important duties are the following:

1. Arrange for the annual planning conference or retreat.

2. Keep going a continuous inquiry to discover and enlist prospective workers — the goal being a leadership *two deep* for every position in the church.

3. Constantly inform workers of leadership training opportunities such as: (*a*) summer schools and conferences; (*b*) community leadership training schools; (*c*) workshops, institutes, round tables, rallies, etc.; (*d*) correspondence courses.

4. Organize leadership training classes in the local church: (*a*) for cadet or beginning teachers; (*b*) study courses for teachers in service.

5. Keep on file an up-to-date record of church members who are accredited to teach one or more courses. Encourage others to qualify for this service.

6. See that resources available from the denominational Board of Christian Education and the Division of Christian Education, N. C. C. C., are on hand for those who administer and teach in the program of Christian education.

7. Improve the programs of the monthly workers' conference.

8. Provide an adequate workers' library. Encourage all leaders to read books and magazines in the field of their special service or interest.

9. Provide for in-service training of church officers and the superintendent of the church school.

10. Work out a plan of outreach and educational evangelism for the church school.

11. Be on the lookout for resources in the field of audio-visual aids. Discover those who can handle with skill the mechanical attachments used in presenting such aids.

12. Evaluate or measure the effectiveness of the church's program of Christian education by means of an achievement chart.

13. Hold annually a recognition service or banquet for the educational workers in the church.

14. See that accurate and easily interpreted records are kept of enrollment, attendance, and student progress.

How Are Goals to Be Chosen?

Many intelligent people have become impatient with the Protestant church school because its work seemed to be without definite purpose or aim. Goals are important in securing and training volunteer leaders. Respect and enthusiasm are kindled by an impression that we know what we want and where we are headed. Each church should work out for itself the aims of its educational program, and these aims should be reached through co-operative thought and discussion.

The task can be broken down and simplified by making special assignments to the various departments and organizations responsible for Christian education in the local church. Each one of these agencies should choose its own objectives and submit them for criticism to the general workers' conference. The members of the latter, having passed through this experience, are ready to set up aims for the church's comprehensive program of Christian education. Once these are agreed upon, the goals of the different departments should be revised by the entire group, so as to bring them in line with the over-all purposes of Christian instruction and guidance in the life of the church. The final step is to present the results of these labors in co-ordinated form to the regularly constituted Board of Christian Education for approval or suggested revision.

When goals have been finally adopted, they should be presented and explained to the congregation. Many churches fail to make satisfactory progress in their attempts at Christian nurture because they do not enlist the general understanding and support of their members in this great venture. Sermons by the pastor from time to time and constant use of the weekly bulletin will help to publicize the direction in which the program of Christian education is moving.

Following is an illustration from the "Permanent Goals" adopted by the church school of the First Presbyterian Church, Evanston, Illinois:

Goals for the Entire Church School

1. By the time a student completes the senior year in the high school department, it is planned that he will have attained:

   a. A growing appreciation for and participation in the worship of God.

   b. A knowledge of the Bible that will include at least these things:

     (1) A thorough knowledge of the life of Christ.

     (2) A study of the Old and New Testaments, with a knowledge of the content of each.

     (3) An appreciation of the types of Bible literature: poetry, wisdom, law, history, devotional material.

     (4) Memorized passages of spiritual value.

     (5) A study of the Prophets.

     (6) A familiarity with the books of the Bible.

     (7) The letters of Paul.

   c. A *working* knowledge of Protestant Christianity: its history and modern meaning for us (including such things as a knowledge of symbolism and a familiarity with the Westminster Catechism).

   d. An appreciation of Christian social ethics and of the impact of the Church upon world conditions; alcohol education; a Christian approach to the problems of war and peace and international affairs; race relations; economic justice; Christian citizenship; etc.

   e. A progressive and thorough study of missions, particularly in connection with the Youth Budget, through which our church school gives. A knowledge of where our Church-supported missionaries are located, showing how this fits into the larger picture of world Christianity.

2. In the student's *personal* religious life and growth:

    a. He learns how to pray naturally, without embarrassment; also cultivates the discipline of daily Bible-reading.

    b. He is led by parents, teachers, and ministers to a commitment to Christ and to his teachings and example.

    c. Every student in the church school is given some opportunity to know what the Church has to offer him in life work. A church ought to send out *at least* one person into the work of the Christian Church each year.

    d. Each student progressively acquires a conscientious attitude about his own stewardship — the giving of his time, talents, and material resources — for the work of the Christian Church. Along with this should be a respect for church property and a reverence for the building that precludes rowdyism.

    e. That a student may have an opportunity to know what morality is under the guidance of Christ, a church school should point up a Christian standard of ethics for all its students, so that they can measure their own conduct and grow in character development.

3. That we in the church school enable children and young people to come to a well-rounded Christian personality in every way we can: by counseling, by teaching, by example, and by providing social and workmanship opportunities.

4. The church school should constantly strive to raise its standards, keeping aware of the latest trends in Christian education.

5. The P.T.A. should strive to plan an increasingly influential part in more effective parent-teacher-student relationships.

6. The church school library and visual aids should be used more fully by parents, teachers, and students.

The Evanston Church also adopted goals for parents and teachers, and for each department of its educational program.

Can We Plan for a Year at a Time?

Dr. Weldon Crossland, pastor of the great Asbury-First Methodist Church of Rochester, New York, answers this question with a ringing affirmative. He maintains, on the basis of wide and successful experience as a Christian educator, that any church school of any size can plan its activities for a twelve-month period.[1]

Advantages of such long-range projection are immediately apparent. The contribution of those chosen to carry the educational work of the church is lifted up and dignified. Leaders are stimulated to analyze the program of Christian education and offer suggestions for improvement. The relationship of the church to the teaching of Christian faith is made clear and emphasized. Problems are mutually shared, resulting in a revelation of the need for patient understanding. Opportunity is present for the acknowledgment and correction of previous mistakes. Frequently, in the helpful atmosphere of earnest discussion, unsuspected leadership is discovered. Important events and dates take their proper place in the general church calendar. Best of all, as workers wrestle with their responsibility for teaching Christian truth, they come to see how necessary is their continued growth by means of "in-service" training.

Surely there can be little argument about the value of planning for a year ahead. But how to do it? The educational work of the church has been done in haphazard, hit-or-miss fashion for so long, that the idea of systematic projection seems to be a radical departure from the customary procedure. We ignore the fact that businessmen and labor groups have mastered the techniques of long-range planning. The pastor and officers of the church are compelled to think in terms of a budget for at least a year. There is no sensible reason why the church school and its allied activities should stumble along from week to week. Many church schools plan their programs on a definite basis for a year, and less definitely for more than a year.

The writer knows of a congregation that provides a week-end retreat — Friday evening to Sunday morning — at a well-appointed summer camp, to set up the church's program for the subsequent twelve months. Ministers, church officers, and church school staff sit down together, talk over their problems, and assign specific

[1] *How to Build Up Your Church School*, pp. 129–140. Abingdon-Cokesbury Press.

functions in terms of objectives agreed upon for the year. This retreat is a wonderful experience, which has completely "made over" the church in question as a fellowship of believers and a spiritual force in the community.

Many churches perhaps would have to put on a less expensive type of planning program. But whatever form the conference may take, it should meet at the earliest possible date in September, if not in the spring or early summer. Invitations with return postals should be issued well ahead of time to those who are expected to attend. A further check of their attendance by phone during the two days immediately preceding the date is advisable. Careful preparation for the meeting is essential, covering topics to be discussed, time schedule (leaving certain periods for questions and comments from the floor), and specific assignment of duties to those who are to take the lead.

Suggested Steps in This Procedure

1. Appointment of a committee from the workers' conference to plan with the board's committee on leadership education.

2. It would be the responsibility of this joint committee, in consultation with the pastor and church school superintendent, to:

a. Explore the plans and emphases of the denominational Board of Christian Education so as to give these projections proper emphasis in the work of the local church.

b. Set up the program of the annual planning conference, which should provide opportunity for: a review and critique of the past year; choice of goals for the next twelve months; discussion of practical ways and means of achieving these objectives; suggesting the budget needed to carry on the church's educational activities; deciding upon the chief dates-events in the Christian education calendar for the year; brief periods of devotional refreshment, recreation, and fellowship. Except in the case of very small churches, there would be need of both general and departmental meetings in a conference of this kind.

c. Determine the date and the place of the planning conference; send out proper notices.

d. Secure the consent and preparation of those who are to appear on the program.

e. Co-ordinate the findings of the conference and report to the board of Christian education.

3. Appointment of a committee from the board of Christian education to take the report of the conference and prepare a calendar for the year ahead, including a brief statement of goals and a schedule of dates-events.

a. It would be the duty of this committee to give adequate publicity to this calendar.

The following is a sample of a calendar outlining a continuous program of leadership education for the local church, which is suggestive, but of course incomplete: [2]

AUTUMN

Small Church	*Large Church*
Annual Recognition and Dedication Service	Annual Recognition and Dedication Service
Christian Education Week Observed	Christian Education Week Observed
Monthly Workers' Conference	Monthly Workers' Conference
Participation in a Standard Training School	Standard Training School
Weekly Training Class as a Part of Sunday Church School Program	Weekly Training Class as a Part of Sunday Church School Program
Acquaint Workers with Home Study Plan	Acquaint Workers with Home Study Plan

WINTER

Monthly Workers' Conference	Monthly Workers' Conference
Weekly Training Class as Part of Sunday Church School Program	Weekly Training Class as Part of Sunday Church School Program
Home Study	Home Study
Emphasize Reading	Emphasize Reading
Books on Missions	Books on Missions
Books on Christian Education	Books on Christian Education
Missions	*Missions*
Baptist Leader	*Baptist Leader*

[2] *Training Leaders for Your Church*, A Program of Leadership Education for Local Baptist Churches. American Baptist Publication Society.

Small Church

School of Missions or a Conference on Missions

Large Church

Midweek Night Training School with Classes to Meet the Particular Needs of the Local Church. Consider a School of Missions

SPRING

Monthly Workers' Conference

Midweek Night Class on Church Membership and Baptist Beliefs

Home Study

Plan for Christian Education Week

Monthly Workers' Conference

Home Study

Weekly Training Class as Part of Sunday Church School Program

Plan for Christian Education Week

SUMMER

Monthly Workers' Conference

Home Study

A Training Class Within the Vacation Church School

Assemblies, Camps, and Conferences

Summer Leadership Training Schools

Monthly Workers' Conference

Home Study

Weekly Training Class as Part of Sunday Church School

A Training Class Within the Vacation Church School

Assemblies, Camps, and Conferences

Summer Leadership Training Schools

CHAPTER III

RECRUITING LEADERSHIP

"How do you go about getting a new teacher for the Sunday school?" asked the church school superintendent of the visiting minister from another town.

"We usually begin with prayer," said the preacher.

"I know," Mr. Jones replied. "We pray from time to time about such matters, but I was thinking of the more practical steps. After all, someone has to be on hand next Sunday for that class of boys in the basement."

"Our experience has shown," said the minister, "that prayer is the first and most essential step, if we want to get the right person for the job. To begin with, it lifts this important quest out of the realm of mere formality or begging around. In the second place, it arms those chosen to approach the prospect with a call from God and the Church. This gives the whole procedure an atmosphere of dignity commensurate with the supreme importance of the task he is asked to consider. I think you will understand if I tell you what we do.

"We have a committee of our board of Christian education on staff personnel. This committee keeps an up-to-date list of potential church workers based on a continuous survey of our educational needs and the talents present in the congregation. The minister sits down with the staff committee for a review of this roster. Qualifications and interests of each person on it are carefully recorded opposite the name. As the chairman runs down the list, quite a number of names can be almost automatically eliminated, because the record shows that they do not fit the picture of the vacancy. Perhaps at the end of half an hour some eight or ten real prospects have been singled out and their names placed upon the blackboard.

"Then the group engage in a period of earnest, silent prayer that God will lead them to choose the person of his own preference for the responsibility under consideration. The minister, or someone designated by him, closes the prayer session by voicing audibly the desires of those present. Then a gradual elimination of names takes place until a unanimous decision is reached as to the person who should be challenged with the opportunity for service.

"Further recourse to prayer is had as to who should be asked to approach the prospect. We always send two people, because it shows that we really mean business and they can support each other in presenting the cause. Our purpose is to find *the* two persons connected with the official life of the church, who are likely to have the greatest influence on this particular prospect. The group then ask God to guide those chosen to represent them in the appeal that they make. If the one to be visited is informed of this cumulative spiritual experience through which the group has passed in reaching its decision, he is bound to be impressed with the sincerity and the urgency of the call. He realizes that the church does not look upon Christian education as a side line, but as a glorious opportunity to bring in the Kingdom of God. Sometimes we fail. But usually we get the man or the woman we want."

"You have given me some interesting ideas," Mr. Jones remarked, "but there are several questions I should like to ask. Somehow, I have a feeling it is not so easy as it sounds."

"There is nothing easy about it," Dr. Strong replied. "Shoot your questions. I'll do the best I can to answer them."

"Well, in the first place, you spoke of a continuous survey of committee needs and congregational resources. How do you make this survey and how do you keep it up-to-date?"

"A complete answer to your question involves the work of two committees. The first is the one on outreach. Making use of the suggestions contained in the materials of the National Christian Teaching Mission,[1] it keeps track of the people moving in and out

---

[1] These may be obtained by writing to Dr. Harry H. Kalas, National Christian Teaching Mission, 206 S. Michigan Avenue, Chicago 4, Illinois.

of the community and of trends in population growth. It invites new residents to become members of our church school, and notifies the proper departments of prospective increase in enrollment.

" The other committee is the one on staff personnel. One of its chief functions is to discover potential leaders for positions of responsibility in the church. Of course, each individual member of this committee is constantly on the prowl for likely prospects. But last year it made its contribution more comprehensive and effective by using a church talent survey or questionnaire. I shall be glad to send you a copy of the instrument if you wish. In this connection I should say that many churches are using the Christian Service Registration Card, which has been produced cooperatively and may be obtained from the Division of Christian Education, N. C. C. C." [2]

The form that Mr. Jones received is shown on pages 36, 37.

" This committee on staff personnel canvassed the needs of the program first with the committee on outreach. Then it distributed the survey blank at a Sunday morning service, afterward securing a supplementary distribution through the various adult organizations of the church. After the blank was carefully interpreted, the pastor co-operated by stressing the importance of filling in the questionnaire. When the returns were tabulated, twenty-eight groups of prospective leaders were discovered. Later we reduced this number to nine classifications with certain subheads. The names secured were carefully listed, with a brief biographical sketch for each one. Later these people were followed up in personal conference. So you see we have a real basis on which to ask for God's help. We have been doing some work ourselves.

" Another good way to discover talent for use in the work of the church is described in a leaflet put out by the Division of Christian Education, N. C. C. C. I cannot remember the exact title.[3] But I can give you the plan in substance. A committee on personnel, similar to the one we have in our church, is appointed by the

[2] Department of Leadership Education, Division of Christian Education, National Council of the Churches of Christ in the United States of America, 206 S. Michigan Avenue, Chicago 4, Illinois.

[3] *How to Find Teachers and Leaders,* by Paul H. King. Division of Christian Education, N. C. C. C.

Volunteer Service Enlistment Blank

Every Christian called to serve
Every worker called to prepare

As evidence of my loyalty to Christ as my Saviour and Lord, and of my willing-
ness to assume my share of responsibility in the task of:

Reaching others for Christ
Teaching others so that they may come to know Christ
Winning others to Christ
Enlisting others in service for Christ
Training others to render more effective service for Christ

**I INDICATE BELOW THE FIELDS OF SERVICE IN WHICH I WILL CONTINUE
TO SERVE, OR FOR WHICH I WILL PREPARE TO SERVE AS CALLED UPON.**

Signed _____

Address _____ Phone _____

Mark the appropriate columns with (x) to indicate necessary data

	EXPERIENCE		NOW DOING	NEED HELP	WILLING TO PREPARE
	CONSIDERABLE	SLIGHT			
CHURCH ADMINISTRATION					
Deacon or Deaconess					
Trustee					
Board of Christian Education					
Music Committee					
Other church committee					
Church officer					
EDUCATIONAL LEADERSHIP					
Teach a class of:					
Children					
Youth					
Adults					
Associate teacher					
Departmental supervision					
Departmental secretary					
Sunday church school officer					
Work with children in expanded session					
Home Department worker					
Vacation Church School					
Weekday Church School					
Leader in Missionary Education					
Leader in Leadership Education					
Librarian					
GROUP LEADERSHIP					
Adult Work					
Men's Council: officer or committee member					

Mark the appropriate columns with (x) to indicate necessary data

	EXPERIENCE		NOW DOING	NEED HELP	WILLING TO PREPARE
	CONSID-ERABLE	SLIGHT			
Woman's Society: officer or committee member					
Parent-Teacher groups					
Young Adult Fellowship					
Youth Work					
B.Y.F. officer or committee member					
Adult leaders of youth					
B.Y.F. Adviser					
World Service Counselor					
Student Counselor					
Boys' Group Leader					
Girls' Group Leader					
Children's Work					
Junior Society leader					
Cubs' leader					
Brownies' leader					
Fellowship Worker					
Plan socials					
Direct games					
Plan special programs					
Lead group singing					
Craft activity					
GENERAL CHURCH SERVICE					
Sing in choir					
Usher					
Play piano					
Special music: Vocal____; Instrumental____					
Serve in nursery during church hour					
Home visitation					
Clerical work					
Publicity					
Secretarial work					
Work with audio-visual equipment					
Manual labor					
Through community agencies					
Ministry to needy groups in community					

Persons filling out this Enlistment Blank are not guaranteed an opportunity to serve in their chosen fields, but as seems wise may be called upon for services where and when needed.

Division of Education in Home, Church, and Community of the American Baptist Convention
1703 Chestnut Street, Philadelphia 3, Pa.

[4] May be obtained from the Board of Education and Publication of the American Baptist Convention, 1703 Chestnut Street, Philadelphia 3, Pennsylvania.

board or committee on religious education. Its first responsibility is to make a survey of staff needs for the entire educational program of the church. The jobs thus revealed are carefully listed and mimeographed according to various age levels.

" The second step is to determine how many organizations there are in the church among whose membership there might be hidden talent for educational tasks. The personnel committee then invites two representatives of each of these organizations to meet with it. They are requested to bring the roll of their group. The purpose, of course, is to examine carefully the names thus submitted for prospective leadership. If the church is small, one or two meetings of the committee will suffice to complete the inventory. In a larger church, it may have to meet on several different evenings to do a thorough job.

" Experience shows that a carefully planned procedure for a meeting of this kind contributes substantially to achieving the goal of the joint endeavor. For example, a program somewhat like the following, keeps people on the track and gets definite results:

" An opening devotional period is led by the minister, the director of religious education, or the general superintendent of the Sunday school.

" The purpose of the meeting is explained by the chairman of the committee, and the responsibility of the organizations represented is briefly outlined.

" Specific needs are presented with the distribution of mimeographed sheets showing immediate and calculated future openings.

" The plan of discovering potential leadership is shared.

" Class and organization membership rolls are then examined. Each person in a specific group is evaluated as a potential worker in the church.

" From this experience a prospect list for future personal contact is compiled.

" Definite assignments are made for interviewing the people thus accepted, and their names are recorded on cards for a permanent file.

" Carefully chosen representatives are briefed on their approach to each of these individuals. The purpose of this initial visit is to get them to agree that their names may remain in the leadership pool.

" A plan is then agreed upon for reporting back to the personnel committee.

" Interesting revelations come to light through the efficient work of a committee such as this. Usually the discovery is made that there are ample resources available in the church for offering the educational opportunities that the congregation ought to enjoy. Under the guidance of God's Spirit this has always been true down through the years in Protestant communions. An intelligent approach to the problem verifies the fact for our own time.

" People are challenged and greatly encouraged by the idea that they can render an important service in other ways than teaching a class, although we are usually after instructors. Secretaries; pianists; workers with crafts, audio-visual aids, dramatics, Boy and Girl Scouts, recreation; mechanics; cooks; and a host of other talented workers may be enlisted by the systematic investigation of a personnel committee. Highly skilled people are discovered and used, who may not be able to undertake a formal assignment but who can make a significant contribution for a short period of time, or who may serve in an advisory capacity.

" Let me give you two other sources of practical suggestion as you face the problem of securing leaders for the task of Christian education.[5] You will be amply repaid by summarizing the content of each pamphlet and testing out some of the ideas they advance."

Mr. Jones ordered the materials and gave them careful study. He jotted down the following suggestions for discussion at a subsequent workers' conference:

" 1. Co-operate with the pastor in securing proper information from new members received into the church.

[5] *So You Want Inspired Teachers,* by H. J. Sweet. Division of Christian Education, N. C. C. C. *If You Want Teachers,* by Erwin L. Shaver. Division of Christian Education, N. C. C. C.

" 2. Stimulate the minister to keep the congregation informed from the pulpit regarding the needs and the supreme importance of Christian education.

" 3. Dignify the call to volunteer leadership. Make it clear that one is highly honored when he is asked to have a part in transmitting the heritage of a free religion.

" 4. Arrange to have the benediction of the church bestowed upon those who agree to undertake a specific educational task, with public pledge of support from the congregation. Samples of dedication or installation services may be obtained from denominational headquarters or from the Division of Christian Education, N. C. C. C.

" 5. Consider the possibility of a 'teachers' compact' — a covenant listing certain obligations on the part of the worker and the mutual promises of help, encouragement, and appreciation from the church.

" 6. Provide basic training and guidance on the job through supervision, suggested reading, and leadership education in the local church as well as in community classes.

" 7. Give those chosen for this task tools with which to work — equipment, maps, commentaries, a library, etc. Dr. Sweet says in his little pamphlet: 'Equipment alone does not make a school. But there is no excuse for not doing the best possible with what we have. Just plain good housekeeping in the house of the Lord is often what is needed most. There are few churches that cannot be clean and comfortable and beautiful in simple ways. Screens, blackboards, bulletin boards, and storage facilities are possible. If you cannot afford to buy, build these things yourselves.'

" 8. Plan for occasions of appreciation and fellowship, culminating in an annual banquet or picnic, in honor of the Christian education staff.

" 9. Strive to generate a spirit of friendly understanding and co-operation in all educational activities of the church. People like to work in groups where they have a hand in shaping policies, and where those in charge make requests rather than give orders.

" 10. Find a way to serve the personal and spiritual needs of teachers and other workers. The minister and the general superintendent have a wonderful opportunity here in the role of counselor and friend. We all need encouragement at times, and fresh spiritual insights.

" 11. Make available training opportunities outside the church. A budget appropriation to help with the expense of attending a Summer Leadership Training School, or some stimulating ' Workshop,' will pay handsome dividends.

" 12. Present a special appeal to the older group of young people and to the young adults. Help them to organize a training class for cadet teachers. While these candidate teachers are taking their work, they also have an opportunity for observation of the regular instructors and for substitute teaching under guidance."

Mr. Jones worked that preacher for all he was worth during the week he spent at his house. His next question was, " How do you present this call you have been talking about to the person you want to enlist? "

" We approach the individual we hope to reach with a businesslike proposition, but in the spirit of prayer.

" First of all, we hand him a blueprint of the job he is asked to undertake. Let us say that we are seeking a teacher for the church school. It is only fair that the person involved should be informed:

" 1. Regarding the needs and the difficulties of the group he is asked to handle, as well as their potential assets.

" 2. That there will be lessons to prepare, which require more than an hour on Saturday night or Sunday morning, if they are to be taught effectively.

" 3. That his contacts with the class should go beyond the period of formal instruction on Sunday into the sharing of life in recreation, personal counseling, and service projects.

" 4. That the church school is operated on the basis of a plan, and that teachers work together with other members of the staff to attain certain common goals and purposes. This involves accurate records and regular reports, prompt attendance, and willing participation in the training program of the local church.

" 5. That the life and example of the good teacher is often more powerful than his class contribution. Hence, he is expected to be loyal to the work of the church, to its ordinances, and above all, to its founder, Jesus Christ.

" This looks like a large order, but there is really nothing unreasonable in its demands. And we have found that worth-while people like to know that the church means business.

" Having described the task, we then reveal the manner in which we were led to choose his name from the general list. Our conviction is recorded that this is a call from God and the church to a definite responsibility and our hope that he will consider it prayerfully. We make it clear that we are not there merely to get someone to take an assignment, but because we believe he is the best qualified person to do the job. Such an approach lifts the visit into its true perspective of spiritual search, and avoids appealing to unworthy motives. It short-circuits petty objections and prolonged argument.

" The appeal itself is based on a few simple propositions emphasizing the importance of the church school teacher's opportunity, namely:

" 1. A world in chaos needs the teachings of Jesus as never before in the history of man.

" 2. Our physical survival, as well as our moral and spiritual health, depends upon an acceptance and practice of Christian truth.

" 3. Volunteer teachers carry the major burden in free Protestant churches of transmitting this saving religious faith.

" 4. Here is your chance to participate in a spiritual enterprise of supreme importance to both individual human beings and society at large.

" Following is a typical ' sales talk ' which has been found successful in 90 per cent of the cases where it was used. Its substance, with minor revisions, is reproduced from Dr. Crossland's book on *How to Build Up Your Church School.*[6]

" We represent the committee on staff personnel of the Sunday school and the church itself. We truly believe that no task is more important today than Christian education in our Protestant churches. In the church school our children, young people, and adults learn to live

[6] *How to Build Up Your Church School*, pp. 44–46.

the Christian life through study, sharing, and fellowship. You and I both know how deeply indebted we are to those church school teachers who have served us in the past.

" There is one class in the senior department of boys and girls who today are without a teacher. Mrs. Johnson, who taught them during the past two years, is moving out of the city. The youngsters of that class are among the most active and interesting in the entire church school. You doubtless know some of them and their parents. This is one of the livest classes we have.

" They are now studying the life of Christ, and are old enough to be keenly interested in his ministry. Last Sunday the title of the lesson was ' The Temptation in the Wilderness.' The Sunday before, it was ' The Baptism of Jesus.' This coming Sunday they will study ' The Choosing of the Disciples.' I have here both the teacher's quarterly and the pupil's study book, which contain a great deal of helpful and interesting material.

" I have come in the Master's name to give you the privilege and opportunity of leading this fine group of boys and girls in their religious study. It is the kind of service Christ rendered the children while he was on earth. You have the personality and talents to do this. You would instantly win the interest and affection of the whole class because of your friendliness and your way with young people. You would represent Christ to them, and, next to their parents, would become their best friend.

" You would render Christ and them a superb service as their leader, and I know that because of your loyalty to Christ and your church you would like to do this. You will be making an outstanding contribution to these boys and girls and to your church as you serve them. You do not now have any other definite responsibility in the church, while there are many members who are caring for several tasks. This is one that I feel you can do better than anyone else in the church. God will richly bless you and give you a deep satisfaction as you give your best to this task."

Mr. Jones's last question was this: " What do you look for in a prospective teacher? What do you hope to find? "

" At this point we try to be thoroughly realistic. While we would like to secure people who have made a special study of both religion and education, we know that any such anticipation is wishful thinking. Most of the folks we will use come to their new responsibilities with very little previous training for the specific task assigned. Perhaps it is better so. Down through the ages God has used plain people to transmit the message of his gospel. Education on the job is the answer to this problem.

"You will understand our position in this matter more clearly if I say that we believe there are certain *essential* qualities for success on the part of a volunteer leader, and if other *desirable* assets are present, so much the better.

Essential Qualifications

"1. Religious devotion — we always want a person who believes in prayer and practices the presence of God — one who lives out his religion in his daily conduct.

"2. Personal attractiveness — we do not necessarily mean the 'glamour type.' But we are thinking of a person who is warm-hearted, outgoing, sacrificial in nature, with a gift for getting along with people.

"3. Intelligence — in this trait the prospect should be above the average of the congregation. We do not expect to get all the high I.Q.'s. There is a question as to whether it would be wise to attempt such a thing, although the brighter the mind, other things being equal, the greater the capacity for leadership. It is certainly true that a person in a position of responsibility should have sufficient intelligence to command respect for his opinions and to provide room for personal growth.

"4. Teachableness — we are thinking here of the humble spirit — the mind which was in Christ Jesus — a good listener; one able to laugh at himself; willing to study and take training.

"We feel that the Christian leader must have these basic qualifications in fair measure, if he or she is to succeed in the service of the Master. It is fortunate for the church if the person chosen also possesses certain other assets mentioned below:

Desirable Qualifications

"1. More than a superficial knowledge of the Bible and other basic religious literature.

"2. Some trustworthy knowledge of psychology — an understanding of how human personality develops.

"3. Creative imagination and resourcefulness in directing the activities of other people.

" 4. Training in educational method and objectives.

" 5. Previous successful teaching experience.

" 6. The know-how of leading others to a personal commitment for Jesus Christ.

" We need to remember that there are certain individuals wholly unfitted for this sacred task, however sincere and earnest may be their desire to serve. Among those about whom we need to raise a finger of caution are the following:

" 1. A person emotionally unstable.

" 2. The man or woman with an ax to grind.

" 3. The incurable controversialist.

" 4. Beware of the person too anxious for a job in the church. The question of motivation is central here, and must be cleared to the satisfaction of all before any commitment is made.

" The fact remains that nearly every church has untapped resources of leadership strength which ought to be discovered and utilized to improve its educational program. Former teachers and administrators, musicians, scoutmasters, mechanics and technicians trained by the Armed Services, wives of certain members of the congregation who have received special training but have never used it before, public-school people now on the job — these are just a few of the possibilities. In one church a high school principal, carefully trained in the field of education and deeply religious himself, sparks the whole program of Christian education. Dr. Crossland [7] is right, with perhaps a very few unusual exceptions, when he says that enough qualified leaders can be found and developed in any congregation to do an effective job of Christian education."

[7] *How to Build Up Your Church School,* p. 39.

Chapter IV

THE WORKERS' CONFERENCE

What is now known as a "workers' conference" has long been a tool of leadership education in the local church. During earlier days it was generally called a "teachers' meeting," and its chief function was a periodic discussion of Sunday school problems. There were times, however, when the meetings degenerated into bull sessions about petty details, a mere listing of sad deficiencies, or gossip about certain problem children on the roll. Little wonder that those asked to undertake responsibilities in the church school frequently countered with the question, "Will I have to attend teachers' meetings?"

However, thoughtful leaders in the field of Christian education made the old teachers' meeting a helpful experience. The modern product of their continued self-criticism and revision is the workers' conference, an organization designed for a more representative group and for definite training objectives. Hence, we may define a workers' conference as a program of regularly scheduled meetings, in which all the church's educational leaders participate. This means that not only are teachers and officers of the Sunday church school included among the members, but also Boy and Girl Scout leaders, advisers of young people's societies, and every other person officially appointed to help in achieving the goals of Christian nurture.

A workers' conference should be carefully distinguished from the general committee or board of Christian education. The board represents the congregation and is responsible for the policies that govern the educational activities of the church. Its job is the organization, administration, and financing of the church's Christian education program. The workers' conference is a unit in this over-all scheme. Education of the leaders themselves is its chief function. It is a means of in-service or on-the-job training. Increasing the spiritual power and the leadership skill of the workers, and thus improving the total efficiency of religious education, is the major concern of the workers' conference. The relationship between it and the board is very much like that which exists between the public-school board and the staff of its schools. The board confers with the workers' conference from time to time for advice and suggestions. The conference frequently discovers needs and makes recommendations to the board.

Dr. Shaver lists certain advantages of the workers' conference as an instrument of leadership training.[1] For one thing, the center of its interest is focused on the specific problems and purposes of the local church. This furnishes a powerful type of motivation to those who plan for and share in the program. Decisions reached usually culminate in prompt action. The carry-over from discussions to reality is immediate and satisfying. The workers' conference is a time-honored institution with the prestige of history and tradition undergirding it. An in-service group of this kind reaches a far larger number of Christian workers than any other agency of leadership improvement. Conventions, schools, community classes, correspondence courses, guided reading, and personal counseling touch only a small number of our Protestant volunteers. For this very reason alone every possible effort should be made to render practical help through the workers' conference. The meetings of the conference can and often do stimulate a rewarding type of fellowship. They promote consecration to the task assigned and build morale, values that are as essential to desirable outcomes in education as knowledge and skills. The servant of the church feels that he is not alone, but is supported by comrades of like mind and purpose. Thus group loyalty or *esprit de corps* is built up, which, under wise guidance, can make the workers' conference a powerful force for keeping the church school on its toes. One of the most useful contributions the workers' conference can make to the educational life of the church is

[1] *The Workers' Conference Manual,* by Erwin L. Shaver, pp. 20, 21. Abingdon-Cokesbury Press.

the help it can render to cadet or apprentice teachers, as well as candidates for other positions. Churches frequently require all such prospective leaders to attend the meetings of the workers' conference regularly.

How shall we describe the program activities of the workers' conference? No arbitrary limitation may be put upon the range of its discussion and investigation. Any problem that impinges upon the tasks committed to its members is germane to its interest. However, it will prosper if it keeps central in its thinking ways and means of improving educational procedures and teaching skill.

It may, for example, conduct a survey: (1) to discover where the church school ranks as measured by the Standard of the Division of Christian Education, N. C. C. C.; (2) to secure information for presentation to the congregation in graphic form under some such title as " Know Your Sunday School " or " This Is Your Church School "; (3) to reveal the evangelistic and spiritual level of the church as judged by the following outcomes: the number of its members each year joining the church; the number entering Church vocations over a given period of time; and the number of new members of the church school secured through the positive outreach of the staff.

The workers' conference may hold an occasional picnic or banquet simply for fellowship and inspiration. A retreat each year, which combines these two with planning activities, is a happy experience.

Following are a variety of features that illustrate the comprehensive character of the training program that may be sponsored by this group:

1. *Round tables* with specialists on different phases of the church's educational purposes. Discussion and experimentation with new techniques, such as the workshop method, visual aids, or visitation in other churches, may prove stimulating. If a visit is to yield dividends, careful advance preparation should be made.

2. *Addresses* by outstanding speakers (few in number and really top-notch people). Anyone invited for this purpose should

come with a definite assignment beforehand, should be strictly limited as to time, and should expect to answer questions at the close of his talk.

3. *Reports* by delegates to conventions, conferences, or institutes; on significant books; on some observation or investigation which a member or members of the group have been commissioned to make.

4. *Discussions* — carefully planned to explore some problem or to supply some information. For example, a panel may be selected to handle certain topics previously listed by the workers.

5. *Demonstrations — exhibits — dramatizations.*

6. *Construction of standards and measurement of success.*

7. *Coaching* — a meeting from time to time, in which more experienced workers offer practical suggestions to beginners or cadet teachers. Work on a program of this kind would have to begin several weeks in advance to avoid vague generalizations and pious advice.

8. *Lesson planning* — quarterly previews on how to handle lesson materials or monthly meetings to plan for the work of each Sunday.

9. *Leadership training classes.* There is some difficulty here, because the time interval between meetings is usually a month or a quarter. Courses also have to be general in nature so as to transcend departmental lines. However, if the course fulfills a genuine need and a skillful instructor can be found, these are not insurmountable obstacles. The conference may agree to more frequent sessions in order to give the training classes right of way and sustained attention. In other words, the course may become a special project. And there are many areas of knowledge in Christian education which all departments should explore together.

A sampling of possible programs for workers' conferences in the form of a calendar is presented below.[2]

September
    Workers' retreat — to outline aims and objectives for the year's educational program; to hear reports from delegates to summer confer-

[2] *And Gladly Serve,* p. 48. Division of Christian Education, N. C. C. C.

ences and to evaluate their recommendations; to plan for the installation of officers; to formulate a workers' covenant.

October — November — December
Plan for: home visiting; how to observe Christmas; stewardship;
service activities in the church; leadership courses by correspondence.

January — February — March
Have discussion in workers' conferences on: missionary education;
the growing worker — use of rating scales; educational evangelism.

April — May — June
Make plans for: home and church co-operation; summertime activities — vacation school, camps, institutes, leadership schools; preparation for special days; planning certain factors of the program for the
next year in view of results during the past year.

July — August — September
The meetings might be devoted to: plans for leadership education;
the church school library; a picnic for all workers; Christian Education Week.

PLANNING AND CONDUCTING THE WORKERS' CONFERENCE

In order to do effective work in any group there must be organization and assignment of responsibility. Elaborate machinery is
neither necessary nor desirable for success in a workers' conference. But at least the following officers and committees would
seem to have legitimate functions:

Officers: president; vice-president; secretary-treasurer
Committees:

1. A program committee which would have the initiative in
planning.

2. A social committee to provide opportunities for fellowship.

3. The executive committee might well be composed of the
officers and the chairmen of the other two committees.

If the number of the group is very small, perhaps most of its
work can be accomplished in a committee of the whole. But here
again there is the risk of wasting time in the consideration of details. Certainly the personnel of officers and committees should be
rotated from year to year.

Long-range Planning

This is the job of the program committee and should be based
as far as possible on the needs and desires of the workers. The

special goals of the Church at large for a particular year will also be a guiding factor. Variety in types of meetings and balance in selection of problems to be considered are desirable criteria in setting up a series of programs for a year. Some provision should be made for departmental meetings at regular intervals. Frequently, half of the total time is allotted for this purpose.

A convenient tool for registering the opinion of every member of the conference, as well as for securing the recommendations of other responsible people, such as the board of Christian education, is a check list of program ideas. As Erwin L. Shaver suggests, " a mimeographed form should be prepared on which subjects or problems may be listed and rated. The form may contain no suggestions at all, allowing the voters to write in their own preferences. Or, it may contain a number of subjects or problems, with space at the end for others to be added by the voter. The rating may be done as indicated." [3]

	Very Important	Important	Of Least Importance	
Topic or Problem One........................	....	....	....	....
Topic or Problem Two, etc.	....	....	....	....
Additional topics I should like to have taken up.	....	....	....	....
....	....	....	....	....
....	....	....	....	....

Final recommendations could be made to the entire group at the workers' retreat in September.

Preparing for Specific Meetings

1. Give ample notice of the time and place. Co-operate with departmental superintendents in getting the folks to attend. The church calendar, posters, and unique invitations are means of advertising. Get someone to take over this task who has a turn for publicity.

2. Choose a leader for the meeting and post that person care-

[3] *The Workers' Conference Manual,* p. 74.

fully on his or her responsibilities. As far as possible, this function should be assigned to different members of the group from time to time. But the person selected must be able to carry on successfully and preside with efficiency.

3. Work for general participation in the program on the part of a goodly number present. Achieving this objective will, to some extent, depend on the type of meeting planned for a particular session. But certainly every effort should be made to prevent two or three dominating personalities from monopolizing the discussion.

4. Prepare an outline of the program with an approximate time schedule, so that the leader and others who are to take part will have clear guidance regarding how the meeting is expected to proceed. Insist on beginning promptly and closing at the time previously agreed upon.

5. Make specific advance assignments so that definite proposals are set before the conference, with certain leaders designated to present them.

6. Make the atmosphere and surroundings as pleasant and comfortable as circumstances will permit. See that necessary materials and apparatus are all on hand and in apple-pie order before the meeting begins, e.g., a movie projector.

7. Arrange for a final checkup of everything on the day the meeting is scheduled.

Success with workers' conferences depends almost entirely on adequate planning in advance. This means, of course, that a leader has been selected who knows how to run the meetings. He must understand where he is headed, upon whom he can call for help in sustaining interest, when to shut off discussion and when to encourage it, and how to develop the spirit of inspiration and fellowship. Above all, he should be able to keep the group moving toward specific practical objectives.

Sample Programs Actually Used in Workers' Conferences

The current trend is toward three types of meetings:

1. General meetings on occasion, for inspiration, learning about matters of common interest, fun and fellowship.

2. Departmental meetings each month, to study the current Sunday school lessons and to plan for a definite period of work in teaching.

3. Combined general and departmental meetings, for an overall view of some topic or problem, followed by a specialized consideration of it on the part of representatives from different age groups.

Program for a General Meeting

PURPOSE — Information, fellowship, and inspiration.
TOPIC — Stewardship in Cozy Corners Church.
6:00–6:45 — Fellowship supper.
Group singing around the tables at close of meal.
6:45–7:00 — Devotions led by secretary of stewardship, Women's Auxiliary.
7:00–7:30 — Showing of the movie *And Now I See*.
This would have to be carefully prepared for — if possible, have a preview in the afternoon.
7:30–8:00 — Report (blackboard presentation) by treasurer of the church, showing:
1. The per capita giving of the denomination in comparison with other Protestant groups.
2. The per capita giving of the local church in comparison with the average for the denomination as a whole.
3. The benevolence quota for each cause accepted by the congregation last year, and how it was arrived at.
4. The amount of the above subscribed and paid.
8:00–8:15 — Discussion, which would begin when the treasurer closed his report, and would continue until adjournment.

A program such as the above would pay more handsome dividends if it were followed soon by a conference of the departmental type for a careful consideration of how to teach the meaning and practice of stewardship at each age level.

Program for a Departmental Meeting

In a Knoxville, Tennessee, church, all the teachers and officers met by departments for forty-five minutes before dinner to discuss their plans for the next unit of work in the Sunday church school. Points of special emphasis had been listed by the director of Christian education. A slip containing these suggestions was handed to each department head.

After dinner and a brief devotional each superintendent shared with the entire group in a minute or two some of the plans made earlier. These were presented in snappy style and the meeting closed on a note of genuine enthusiasm.[4]

Combination of General and Departmental Meetings

Purpose of the Conference

To help teachers of children, young people, and adults to get a comprehensive view of the Sunday school lessons for the next quarter.

To bring about a better understanding of the basic truths and concepts in each unit of the curriculum, and to see them in relation to the total plan.

To stimulate interest in detailed planning for the quarter's work.

Advance Preparation

Plan to hold your conference at least ten days or two weeks before the new quarter begins — as soon as possible after your new literature arrives.

Arrange all details carefully, so that the meeting will not last more than one hour.

Mimeograph, before the meeting, the lesson titles, with their purposes, for January, February, and March.

Program of the Meeting, dividing the hour into two periods:

First Period — not more than 20 minutes for the whole group

Have a " moment of inspiration ": a hymn, a prayer, a poem, or a bit of Scripture.

Read the titles of the lesson units which you have listed on the mimeographed paper; indicate briefly the purpose of each unit.

Call attention to the limited time schedule, and the importance of capitalizing on minutes in both your workers' conference and in the Sunday school.

Second Period — at least 40 minutes

Go directly into departmental conferences — for teachers of children, young people, and adults to plan specifically for their work during the quarter.

MEASURING PROGRESS

A great many provisions for leadership education make little impression because they are not judged by any standard of success or failure. Dr. Shaver has suggested a scale for measuring the quality of workers' conferences. Its chief worth lies in the *sample*

[4] *Exchange of Ideas for Workers' Conferences*, Department of Leadership Education, Presbyterian Church, U. S.

nature of the instrument. If a church would use the scale as a starting point and construct its own guide for evaluating its workers' conferences, the values achieved would be far superior to taking ready-made work of someone else. A committee might well be appointed to undertake this assignment. Then a whole meeting, maybe two, could profitably be devoted to hearing and revising its report.

After all, there are a few acid tests for the vitality of a workers' conference, which are realistic and largely objective. The first is the record of attendance. Some faithful souls, perhaps, will come out of a sheer sense of duty, regardless of program success or failure. But the majority will attend with any high degree of regularity only if they are helped. The second criterion is the carry-over or transfer of suggestions from the conference to the administration and classrooms of the school. When substantial transfer occurs, the practical usefulness of the workers' conference is pretty well proved. Another sign of success is increasing loyalty and consecration on the part of the staff, as evidenced by such things as personal spiritual growth, willingness to call on parents, fewer times tardy or absent, and more time spent in lesson preparation. Finally, we may be fairly certain that the workers' conference is wide awake if there is a growing sense of obligation on the part of the members for making its contribution significant. Is it easy to get a " yes " to a request for service in the organization or appearance on the program? People like to have a stake in a going concern.

Leadership education never registers until it makes a difference in the local church. The workers' conference is the most flexible tool we have for in-service training of volunteer leaders.

Chapter V

LESSON PLANNING

The lawyer, who stays in business, carefully prepares his cases before appearing in court. The successful surgeon checks each step and estimates every possibility before undertaking to operate. Salesmen are briefed on what they should say and the correct approach to a prospect. Public-school teachers must know how to plan lessons before they are licensed by the state to enter the classroom. But workers in the field of Christian education all too frequently come to their tasks with little or no preparation and with only the vaguest idea of what they are supposed to do. A church school teacher, for example, who spends as much as an hour preparing for her Sunday morning class is above the average.[1]

Most of these people are sincere and earnest. A few, perhaps, are indifferent, or make little effort to compensate for deficiencies of time, devotion, and skill. However, the vast majority would gladly do a better job than they are now turning out, if only they knew how. Very few of our volunteer leaders have received any practical help in the art of lesson planning. For this the church itself is largely responsible. Protestant groups, in their training programs, have been long on theory and academic respectability, but short on down-to-earth, how-to-do-it suggestions for a bewildered teacher facing a group of restless youngsters on a specific Sunday morning. The purpose of this chapter is to supply a pattern or framework that will serve as a guide to the teacher on

[1] *Restudy of Religious Education*, p. 63. Presbyterian Church, U. S., Richmond, Virginia.

both long-range planning and lesson preparation from Sunday to Sunday.

The Value of Lesson Planning

No teaching proceeds by inspiration alone. Good teachers are made, not born ready-made. They develop through hard work, careful study, and consistent planning. A blueprint of the experience the teacher hopes to provide for his pupils is just as important as the plan of an engineer for a bridge. Without planned instruction, goals remain vague, procedures are undetermined, materials chosen may or may not minister to the spiritual growth of the students. A lesson plan sets the course, keeps the teacher on the track, and secures adequate time for desirable points of emphasis in the learning activity. Stated another way the teacher prepares:

1. To eliminate aimless haphazard teaching or monotonous routine.

2. To provide thoughtful, deliberate, and therefore better, selection and organization of subject material.

3. To be able to teach easily without forgetting essential points.

4. To tailor the lesson to the needs of each individual pupil.

What Do We Mean by Lesson Planning?

The lesson plan is an instrument to guide both teacher and pupils in their joint quest for insight and mutual understanding. It contains a statement of objectives and the method to be used in realizing these aims. When effectively used it: (a) focuses the attention of the teacher upon desirable changes in the life of the pupil; (b) provides for definite pupil participation in the class experience; and (c) puts the pupil in the center with the teacher in the background as guide and director of the learning process.

In the last analysis, each teacher must develop his own teaching plans, but lesson planning cannot be hit-and-miss. The teacher who has a well-laid schedule of lesson planning, who goes about it carefully and methodically, will, in the long run, be a more effective teacher than he otherwise could be.

Essential Elements in Lesson Planning

Improved church school materials now in use, or on the way, do not lend themselves to haphazard methods of preparation. Consequently, many teachers who have done little planning heretofore are asking if there is a key or procedure that will enable them to solve this problem of preparation for class work. What are the conditions or principles of good lesson planning without waste of time? The scheme and samples that follow provide one answer to this question. Drawing on the experience of skilled educators, the writer suggests a practical approach which has been tested by hundreds of successful teachers in both public and church schools. He was privileged to demonstrate these tools recently in three of the Rocky Mountain states where there are many isolated and poorly equipped Sunday schools. Teachers caught on readily and were able to make practical applications to their own work without great difficulty. Since then he has received copies of lesson plans that have been used, with a new sense of mastery, in all types and sizes of churches.

Below is the key or pattern that contains the elements in successful planning of a specific lesson. It does not show a lesson plan itself, but the main items that go into the procedure of planning at any age level.

1. *Personal spiritual preparation:* Prayer for God's guidance in preparing the lesson and for a ready response on the part of the pupils. This is the most important phase of lesson planning and is never to be omitted or neglected.

2. *Aims or objectives:*
    a. General: To be kept constantly before me for the unit or the quarter.
    b. Specific: To be accomplished in this lesson.

3. *Teaching aids:* The work of helpers, if any, and such materials as maps, posters, charts, models, books, pencils, pictures, magazine and newspaper clippings, etc. For example:
    a. What aids shall I need to tell this story effectively?
    b. What materials shall I need for this special project?

c. What materials shall I need for the dramatization of this incident?

4. *A list of key questions or problems:* These could be problems that the teacher wishes to sharpen for himself or questions to be asked of the pupils. There may be an occasional lesson with no use of a key question, but this is likely to be very rare, and at least some questions should be prepared ahead of time. These are often worked into the outline of procedure.

5. *Outline of teaching procedure:* This involves the development of the lesson for the day and the assignment of future work. Teachers will vary the time and place of the assignment in terms of personal preference and pupil needs. However, the importance of assignments cannot be overemphasized.

a. Steps in teaching the lesson (to be worked out in detail).

b. Assignment of future work: (1) general, to the group as a whole; (2) to individuals or committees; (3) for the co-operation of parents.

(The assignment should be made at the strategic time, be clear, and be designed to motivate pupil interest.)

6. *Time schedule:* The number of minutes allotted to each item in the teaching outline should be carefully estimated. Don't try to cram everything in the magazine into one lesson plan; intentionally, more suggestions are given each week than any one person can use in an hour; so pick out what seem to you the most essential things that you can use in the time you have.

7. *Evaluation or self-criticism:* This comes, of course, after the lesson is taught, and consists of reflection on what happened. Discover your good points and weaknesses in the presentation on each Sunday. Suggestions for improving your teaching should be jotted down as soon as possible; Sunday afternoon is not too soon, while items are fresh in your mind.

Self-evaluation Check List

1. Did I accomplish my aim?
2. Did I relate the teaching clearly to the pupils' everyday living?
3. Did my introduction capture the pupils' attention?
4. Did my key questions arouse good conversation and discussion?

5. Did I remember to call for any assignments or reports I had asked for?

6. Did the pupils use their Bibles?

7. Did I make home assignments and motivate them well?

8. What have I learned, and what better ways will I use next week?

The above is a pattern that may be used in preparing a single lesson by assembling in an orderly way material and notes for use in teaching the lesson. It is not a lesson plan. Items 5 and 6 will be developed in detail in sample lesson plans which follow.

How to Plan a Lesson

1. Read the treatment of the lesson in the teachers' magazine or quarterly, mark carefully the sentences or suggestions that are likely to be most useful in making your lesson plan. (Ideas mentioned in the pattern given above should be most useful in guiding this process.)

2. Study with care the chief Bible passage or passages.

3. Read the assignment in the pupils' book or quarterly.

4. If there are additional materials available, such as a pupils' workbook or activity packet, examine them with a view to determining what use, if any, they may serve in teaching the lesson.

Good teachers will be on the lookout all the time and everywhere for extra resources that will help them to drive home the truth of the Christian gospel. However, because the large majority of Protestant teachers labor in small churches, where little or nothing is supplied in the way of helpful references, the plans that follow use only the Bible and the literature put out by the denominations. They are intended to convey the fact that good teaching can be done within the suggestions offered by the average Protestant communion. Let no one assume, however, that this is a legitimate excuse for neglecting auxiliary tools readily at hand, or easily obtainable, that may be used to enrich his teaching.

Using the foregoing pattern of steps, let us now plan a few lessons at different age levels.

Primary Lesson Plan
The God We Worship

Since this is the first lesson in the fall quarter (October–December, 1949), you will want to read with care the section in the teacher-parent magazine (*Opening Doors* [2]) entitled "Planning Ahead" (pages 24–26). Suggestions regarding the use of general articles and the pupils' activity packet should be faithfully followed. A possible time schedule for your class is also presented.

After seeking God's help, read the following materials:

1. Section in *Opening Doors* that deals with the teaching of this lesson (pages 28–30). Underline significant sentences to which you may wish to give special attention in your planning.

2. Scripture references for this lesson, which are found in the section of the magazine mentioned above: Gen., ch. 12; Ex. 20:3–6.

3. The child's brief reading book, entitled *People of the Promise*. [3]

When we come to the actual lesson outline, the first thing we want to know is what we are trying to accomplish with the children next Sunday. Where are we headed? Therefore, we determine and set down our aims or objectives.

AIMS — GENERAL: An excellent statement is found on page 27 of the magazine. Another, equally good, appears on page 28. It follows: "The boys and girls will learn to understand that as Christians we worship the one true God and that we learn to know him through the Bible."

AIMS — SPECIFIC: 1. To acquaint the children with their new reading books — introduction of the man Abraham. 2. Discuss actual ways in which people worship. 3. Begin with helping them to distinguish between idols and the true and living God. 4. Simple practice in the use of the Bible — finding passages.

AUXILIARY AIDS: Models or pictures of ancient or foreign idols, of an old temple, and of camels; worship materials; pencils; small supply of Bibles for any who may have forgotten theirs on this first Sunday; activity packets; drawing materials.

KEY QUESTIONS: These are found in the magazine *Opening Doors* on page 28 (they concern the nature of idols); page 29 (they deal with pictures No. 1, 13 of *Primary Teaching Pictures*); page 30

[2] For teachers and parents of primary children, "Christian Faith and Life" curriculum, Board of Christian Education of the Presbyterian Church in the U. S. A.

[3] By Elizabeth Honness. "Christian Faith and Life" curriculum, The Westminster Press.

(they develop the idea of making a classroom a better place in which to worship).

OUTLINE OF PROCEDURE: The steps are so clearly sketched in *Opening Doors* for this first lesson that we need to make very little change. Following is a brief summary of the way in which the time is to be spent:

Opening Fellowship (10 minutes)

1. Display of reading books, with models or pictures of idols, etc.
2. Discussion of the nature of this kind of god, with introduction of Abraham, who wanted a better one. 3. Distribution of new reading books.

Teaching Period (15 minutes)

1. (*a*) Reading together the first story in *People of the Promise*. (*b*) Discussion of the ways people have worshiped in the past — talk about how we worship God today.
2. Story: " The Pratts Go to Church."

Special Activities (15 minutes)

1. Suggestions about how to make the primary room or classroom a better place in which to worship.
2. Children draw what the Pratt family did in church.
3. They begin cutting the designs on first activity sheet.

Assignment for Next Week (5 minutes)

1. For everybody — complete the reading book.
2. Appoint certain children to bring flowers or colored leaves next Sunday (suggested in magazine).
3. The envelope to be made during the week with the parents' help (suggested in magazine).

Worship as Outlined on Page 30 of Magazine (10 minutes)

EVALUATION OR SELF–CRITICISM

1. How did this first lesson go?
2. What mistakes did I make?
3. How can I improve the work next Sunday?

In dealing with the lesson for the primary group, we have woven the plan and the process of building it into a single unit. That makes the whole look a little long and complicated. But it also shows where every item in the plan came from and why it occupies the place it does in the total development. Really, if the teacher bears in mind the " Essential Elements " as she reads the discussion of this lesson in the magazine and marks the appropriate pages, the most important part of her task is over when she has finished the article. It always takes a little more preparation for a *first* lesson than for any other.

The time schedule is just a rough guide to keep the instructor on the main track. It should always be subject to flexible adjustment in order to take advantage of any unusual interest the pupils may have in a particular portion of the lesson. Since the interest span of small children is short, five minutes of the hour has been left unassigned for any use the teaching-learning situation may require.

Because our time is brief, several of the suggestions mentioned in the magazine article are omitted from the plan. But still there is probably more material than can be handled in sixty minutes. Every good teacher plans for more than can be covered in a single class session. Development of such a habit gives depth, confidence, and freedom to the teaching experience.

Junior High Lesson Plan

Our approach in planning the second lesson designed for junior highs is a bit different. First comes the outline of the plan itself as the teacher might use it on Sunday morning. Explanations as to how it grew are subscribed in a section that follows.

Why Read the Bible?

Personal Spiritual Preparation — Pray that God will enable me to make clear the need of knowing and understanding the Bible.

AIMS — GENERAL: 1. To show pupils what is the single continuing theme of the Bible. 2. For Unit I of this quarter's material, to teach the purpose and plan of the Bible and show pupils why we read it.

AIMS — SPECIFIC: 1. Help pupils to see that we read the Bible not only for information, but because through it as through no other book, the Spirit of God works to change us into persons fit to live in company with him and with our fellow men. 2. Show how the Bible is different from all other books.

AUXILIARY AIDS: Notebooks, pencils, and paper.

KEY QUESTIONS: These are found at the end of the notebook assignment for the day, and are based on the study and comparison of Luke 18:9–14 with Deut. 6:7–15.

OUTLINE OF PROCEDURE: Follow the suggestions in *Counsel* [4] (October–December, 1949) and devote the major portion of the period to a discussion of the issues raised by the notebook assignment for today.

    Assignment for Next Week (5 minutes)

    1. Ask pupils to read Chapter 3 of *The One Story*. [5]

    2. Designate a pupil to report on the entire reading book.

  [4] For teachers and parents of junior highs, " Christian Faith and Life " curriculum, Presbyterian Board of Christian Education.

  [5] By Hulda Niebuhr. " Christian Faith and Life " curriculum, The Westminster Press.

3. Pupils are to interview their parents to discover what the Bible means to them — see instruction at foot of notebook page.

Teaching Period

1. (20 Minutes) Ask pupils to read and compare the Scripture passages cited in the notebook. Help them to sense the *feeling* of the Pharisee as over against the *feeling* of the publican. Take cues from suggestions in *Counsel* on teaching procedure.

2. (20 Minutes) Have pupils write answers to the four questions that follow the comparison of the Bible passages and discuss with them the meaning of their replies.

EVALUATION OR SELF–CRITICISM

Jot down mistakes and ideas for doing better next time. The assumption has been made in preparing this lesson plan that a worship period of 15 minutes for the whole department would be provided at the beginning of the hour.

Notes on How the Plan Grew

Again the discussion of how to teach the lesson in the magazine is excellent, so that most of the teacher's work is accomplished by a careful reading of the proper section in *Counsel* (the teacher-parent magazine).

1. The statement of *General Aims* is found in the article entitled "Aims for This Year," which immediately precedes the lessons for the quarter.

2. *Specific Aims* are found on page 28 of the magazine.

3. Suggestions for *Assignment of Future Work* appear right at the beginning of the lesson discussion.

4. *Auxiliary Aids* for this lesson are simple, and perfectly obvious as soon as the notebook assignment is read.

5. The *Key Questions* happen, also, to be provided this time by the notebook.

6. The *Outline of Procedure* follows closely the steps suggested in the magazine. This seems altogether desirable because the lesson for October 9 stands as a background for the remaining work of the quarter. Good teachers, however, will often vary from outlines provided by church literature, depending upon the immediate needs of their pupils.

"It must take hours and hours to plan a lesson!" Not at all. Once the technique is mastered, lesson planning saves time for the conscientious teacher. Someone has aptly said that lesson plans function like a set of hangers in your clothes closet. Orderly arrangement and right spacing are the result. Carefully timed experiments have shown that it takes anywhere from one and a half to two and a half hours to plan a lesson for Sunday morning, depending upon the training and experience of the teacher. Who will say this is too much to give in the service of the Master during a whole week? Good teachers always do a great deal more, of their own free will and accord.

Long-range Planning or Previewing

We have dealt first with the preparation of specific lessons, because that is the immediate and most pressing problem faced by the teacher. The successful instructor, however, is always working ahead, thinking of the relation of a particular lesson to others in a given unit, jotting down reminders of helpful suggestions, ideas, and materials which may be used to attain the objectives of an entire quarter's work. The values of long-range planning have been aptly stated in *My Lesson Planning Book*.[6]

" 1. We are all human. Most of us have more demands upon our time than can be met. We must never, in our teaching, get to the point where we ' can't see the forest for the trees.' Long-range planning is the only way we can maintain perspective. Unless we can see clearly the purpose of each Sunday's session in relation to the over-all purpose of the quarter's work, we lose our sense of direction, and the things we do tend to lack significance. It is only as we see how each Sunday's work contributes to the realization of the goals for the quarter that we have a definite sense of direction and a basis on which we can evaluate the results of our work.

" 2. Variety in teaching approach is important in maintaining pupil interest. It is only as we are able to see listed before us the various teaching approaches we plan to make each Sunday in the quarter that we are able to provide for the variety which we seek. Nothing will kill a live, wide-awake class of boys or girls as quickly as monotony.

" 3. The accumulating and securing of teaching aids takes time. If, for instance, we are going to use pictures from a magazine, a quotation from a book, a filmstrip or stereopticon slides, special missionary material or any other recommended material, we must order it well in advance of the Sunday on which we plan to use it, so that it will be on hand when we want it. It is sometimes as important to plan an *ordering* or *assembling* schedule as it is a *teaching procedure* schedule.

" 4. Special assignments or projects frequently take several weeks

[6] Page 5, 1949 issue. Published by the Board of Christian Education of the Presbyterian Church in the United States of America.

to complete. They must be planned for, and assigned, far enough in advance of the date they are to be completed to be sure that they can be completed on time."

Several ingenious devices and techniques have been invented for guiding the teacher in achieving this purpose. One of the most familiar is the " crosshatch " pattern illustrated on the next facing pages, with the Sundays numbered in the left-hand column. Whenever such a scheme is used, teachers will revise it or adjust it to suit their own individual needs. For example, titles of columns may be changed in wording, and the number increased or diminished. The general pattern can be adapted to any type of materials and all sorts of churches. The chart given here is taken from *My Lesson Planning Book* for 1950–1951, published by the Presbyterian Board of Christian Education.

Of course, all the above is merely suggestive. The wide-awake teacher regards it as grist in the mill, portions of which may be used when planning for a specific Sunday. It is merely a convenient tool for collecting, preserving, and classifying resource material ahead of time.

A Sample of Long-range Planning

Another possibility in the realm of long-range planning is submitted on the pages that follow, using the materials of a different denomination.[7] In this case the notes for preliminary preparation were simply written in a notebook, with no division by Sundays. The section we shall treat is taken from the curriculum for seniors — fall quarter. The title on the " Teacher's Guide " and the " Pupil's Quarterly " is " Aims, Motives, and Methods of Modern Missions." The lesson actually taught is number two, " The Social Aim of Modern Missions."

Following is just a sample of the many student activities and discussions which may be developed by asking a few over-all questions about the work of the entire quarter.

I. *Why Foreign Missions?*
    1. Have children ask their parents this question.
    2. Have each pupil write to one of the church's missionaries, making the same inquiry.

              [7] Presbyterian Church, U. S.

3. The teacher may profitably write for additional information to denominational headquarters or the Missionary Division of the National Council of the Churches of Christ.

4. Some good reasons for the mission enterprise:

a. The preservation of our nation and our way of life depends upon the spread of the gospel. (If Russia were Christian instead of Communist, our safety would be secured.)

b. The freedom of mankind rests upon the acceptance and practice of the teachings of Jesus.

c. The great redemptive purpose — to bring the message of salvation into the lives of men and women everywhere.

d. Sheer gratitude — we are Christians because others in years gone by took up the missionary task.

II. *Where Foreign Missions?*

1. Have children bring maps of different sections of the world, and ultimately block out the area where the Presbyterian Church, U. S., is conducting missionary activities.

2. Write to the Missionary Division of the National Council of Churches.

a. To discover areas assigned to different denominations.

b. To find out about great independent mission movements, such as the China Inland Mission, the World-wide Evangelization Crusade, and others.

3. Write to Dr. C. Darby Fulton, Executive Secretary of Foreign Missions, regarding the missionary responsibility of the Presbyterian Church, U. S.

III. *How Foreign Missions?*

1. Secure material (C. Darby Fulton) on different phases of the missionary venture — evangelistic, medical, educational, agricultural, and industrial.

2. How are missionaries chosen and prepared? Most youngsters do not know that they are the cream of American intellectual and spiritual leadership.

3. How are missionaries supported in their work?

4. How do missionaries carry on their duties? (Some students might write to missionaries, asking them to give a typical day out of their lives.)

IV. For special reports assign to various students biographical sketches of such great leaders in the mission field as:

1. Hudson Taylor, Carey, Morrison, DuBose, Grenfell, and Myers (the past).

2. Kagawa, Schweitzer, Patterson, and Wilson (today).

The above by no means exhausts the possibilities for special projects and topics of collateral interest which may be used as

Planning for Christian Faith and Life,

UNIT I — THE

Junior
Basic Materials: Bible, reading book—*The King Nobody Wanted*, Junior Workbook, teacher-parent magazine—*Discovery*, hymnal—*Hymns for Junior Worship*.

WEEKS	PURPOSE	BIBLE REFERENCES	STORIES & PICTURES	HYMNS
1	To discover the daring dream of Jesus for a Kingdom of love on earth. To become acquainted with church school materials.	*Matt. 28:18-20.* References on pp. 191, 192 in reading book.	"The Young Man with a Daring Dream," p. 31 in *Discovery*. Pictures of life of Jesus and life in Palestine.	Prelude . . . . .144 Response . . . . .134 Hymn . . . . 79 Offering 128
2	To discover that people who believe in the daring dream of Jesus are bringing the Kingdom of God near. This includes children.	*Luke 10:25-37.* the Good Samaritan, p. 132 in reading book. *Josh. 1:9; John 15:12, 13; Rom. 8:35-37; II Tim. 2:3, 15; Ps. 90:17.*	"A Pick and Shovel Army," p 34. A picture of the Good Samaritan.	Prelude . . . . .143 Hymn . . . . 9 Offering . . . . .128 Hymn 79
3	To discover that the Kingdom of God is in our own community and to learn what our part in it is. To guide boys and girls in growing toward Christian citizenship.	*Luke 10:25-37; Ps. 1: 33; 67,* for home reading. (See pp. 37, 38 in *Discovery*.)	"Citizens Remade," p. 37. A picture of the Good Samaritan.	Prelude . . . . .145 Hymn . . . . 23 Offering . . . . .128 Hymn 107
4	To help the Juniors discover that God's Kingdom is for all the world and that they have a part in it.	*Acts 17:24-27; Rom. 10:12-15; Matt. 22:37-39; 28:19,20; Gen. 1:1, 2,31; Ps. 8:24:1,2; 67; I John 3:11; 2:11.*	A legend, "The Bunch of Sticks," p. 40. "Denmark Sets an Example," p. 39. U.S. and Canada have peace, p. 39.	Prelude . . . . .142 Hymn . . . . 90 Offering . . . . .128 Hymn 89

"Education is a shared experience that is active."
This is just one way to plan ahead and see what you are doing in your Sunday

a Program for Church and Home

KINGDOM OF GOD

Schedule: 20 min., activities
25 min., class groups
15 min., worship

PURPOSE: To find out what it means to be a citizen of God's Kingdom;
to become a part of the Kingdom of God, in spirit, word, and action.

OTHER MATERIALS	KEY QUESTIONS FOR PUPIL DISCUSSION	·ACTIVITIES	
		AT CHURCH SCHOOL	AT HOME
Explore materials that will make Jesus real to the child: map of Palestine; globe; New Testament curios.	Who was the king nobody wanted? Why such a title? What was his daring dream? Do you know of others who have had daring dreams?	Plan notebook cover. Explore book *The King Nobody Wanted*. Choose committees: membership, library, research, worship. "Day by Day" and "Discoveries."	Read book at home Bring any curios and pictures.
Paper for bookmarks. Paper for book, cover, crayons, scissors, rulers, pencils. Material for altar cloth, paint, screen, etc.	What was the pick and shovel army? Who was the leader? Why did he organize this army? Who belonged? What did they do?	Make bookmarks, p. 2 in *Junior Workbook*. Instructions for making shelf, p. 28. Begin map of Palestine.	Make a list of others who also had a daring dream and did something about it in our community.
Flag of U.S. Christian flag.	What do we owe the Jewish people? What did they give us? What do the Negroes give us? the Chinese? the red men?	Rehearse choral reading of *Ps. 67*. Finish booklets. Read and dramatize story of Good Samaritan. Work on map of Palestine.	P. 8 in booklet "Discoveries." Library committee to bring book on world friendship.
Globe; map of North America showing Mexico. Curios from Mexico. Books on world friendship.	How do we sometimes treat peoples of other races and nationalities? What can we do to help us live together in one world? What did Jesus say?	Choral reading of *Ps. 67*. Begin research on Mexico. "Day by Day," p. 10. Learn *I John 3: 18*. Work on map of Palestine.	Bring Mexican curios. Begin research on Mexico.

church school work with fourth-, fifth-, and sixth-grade children. It is merely illustrative and is based on the first-year theme, "Jesus Christ."

[13]

the work of the quarter develops. The discerning teacher will think of many more, and adapt them to the particular situation and group for which she is responsible. Of course, they are to be worked into the regular lessons at appropriate spots to stimulate interest and promote pupil participation.

At this point the " old hand " at the business would remind us that no one can do lesson planning for another. It is true that worth-while achievement in this field results only from individual effort. We can help people to learn how to plan lessons, but they cannot take our plans and use them successfully. If teaching is to be truly fruitful, the instructor must do his own reading, thinking, and arranging. The scheme for a class period that comes out of this exercise is likely to be very personal and unique.

Uniformity in style or type of lesson plan is neither possible nor desirable. Lesson plans were never intended to be followed slavishly. They are designed for two chief purposes. One is that the teacher will always give thoughtful and systematic preparation to his work. The other is to insure a desirable arrangement and proper emphasis upon the most important truths to be taught within the time of the lesson period. The specific pattern of lesson planning will vary tremendously from teacher to teacher, and should.

CHAPTER VI

LEADERSHIP EDUCATION COURSES IN THE LOCAL CHURCH

Leadership training classes in the local church are a familiar story. They trace back to the time of Christ in his guidance of the Twelve. Great Protestant leaders, like Calvin and Wesley, have constantly emphasized this method of preparing volunteer workers. The advantages are obvious. One is the fact that courses can be chosen to meet local needs and adapted to individual differences. A strong appeal to local pride and loyalty is possible. The convenience of a relatively small group with a single purpose simplifies administration. The chief difficulty lies in securing adequate leadership for such classes and projects. But if the minister is discharging his obligation as Christian educator, there are no insurmountable obstacles.

Today many such courses are offered for credit. A far larger number, however, are organized to meet a special need in a particular church, without any thought of formal recognition for the work done. Classes for the improvement of leaders in the local church are taught by all kinds of instructors. Most frequently the pastor is the teacher, and this is a good sign for reasons previously stated. However, the general superintendent, the director of Christian education, a public-school person, a college professor, or some specialist — in audio-visual aids, for example — within or without the congregation, may be chosen for the task. Local churches tend to forget or ignore the human resources available for this purpose, either in their own membership or in the immediate neighborhood.

Because of their almost infinite variety, leadership classes in the local church are not easily pigeonholed. They tend, however, to fall into two broad classifications: those designed for apprentice or cadet teachers and workers, and those offered for leaders already in service. In either case, if credit is desired for completion of the required work, the program of the Division of Christian Education, N. C. C. C., should be studied carefully. Following is a summary of its offerings in this field as described in its publications.[1]

Opportunities for Study

The Standard Leadership Education Curriculum has been developed over the years by the various Protestant Churches and interdenominational councils working together. It provides courses on three levels.

First Series courses are designed in general for two types of persons: 1. Those who are ready to take some first steps in training for leadership and/or who need a simplified type of text material as they take these first steps. 2. Those who are for one reason or another able and willing to give only a limited amount of time in this type of formal training.

Second Series courses are designed in general for two types of persons: 1. Those who are ready to take some next steps in training for leadership, and/or who are ready to use an advanced type of text and reference material. 2. Those who are able and willing to give a sizable block of time to this type of formal training.

For a full statement on First Series work, see Educational Bulletin 501. It may be briefly stated that each First Series course is half as long as a Second Series course and that other requirements are correspondingly reduced. Information on Second Series courses is in Bulletin 502.

Third Series courses are designed for persons who have made considerable progress in leadership, who are ready for more specialized work than is involved in the Second Series, and who would welcome opportunity for work suited to their talents and experience. Each Third Series course involves a minimum of thirty hours of work. For a full statement, see Educational Bulletin 503.

A *Manual for Deans* is available for an individual or a board of managers responsible for classes or schools. All courses in leadership education should be a combination of materials and methods; a background course should include some guidance in teaching procedure, while a course on methods should include definite references to con-

---

[1] Bulletins 501, 502, 503. Division of Christian Education, N. C. C. C., 206 S. Michigan Avenue, Chicago 4, Illinois.

tent. Every effort should be made to relate each course to actual work in Christian education through planning, observation, and practice on the part of the students. A limited number of basic courses have been selected by the Division of Christian Education and listed in the Bulletins and in the leaflet with the title *Begin with These*. The local church committee on leadership education should make these basic courses available to the workers early in their program of training, adding others as the need arises.

For further information write to the Department of Leadership Education of the Division of Christian Education, N. C. C. C., or your denominational headquarters.

Courses for Prospective Workers — Apprenticeship

The value of combining theory with practice has long been recognized. People learn by doing under proper guidance. At the same time they are given the philosophy and content background which must undergird the whole process. A class of cadet teachers, for example, continuously operated, may be required to take a certain number of basic leadership training courses before assuming full responsibility of a job in the church. Concurrently its members have opportunity for observing work of the regular instructors in the church school and for substitute teaching followed by evaluation. Candidates for other types of church leadership will profit from taking these general courses, while they are also learning on the job. Churches that contain a program of this kind are seldom without trained leaders to meet the various demands of Christian education. But success in such an experience is possible only if the local church takes its educational task seriously.

It is desirable, although not necessary, that classes for apprentice workers and teachers meet during the Sunday morning church school period. This affords ample opportunity for co-ordinating the academic work with practical experience. Titles of courses that may well be taken by this group include the following from the Standard Leadership Curriculum:

*The Program of My Church — 130a. The purpose of such a course is to give those being trained a survey of the functions of Christian education and how it is organized in their own church. The denominational manual or handbook on this topic should be a part of the class material.

*Introduction to the Bible — 120a or 120b. Since the core of our faith is to be found in the Scriptures, these beginners need an introductory course on the nature and message of the Bible, with suggestions as to how to teach it.

The Life of Jesus — 124a. A biographical study, well handled, can make the teachings of Jesus more attractive and compelling.

My Christian Beliefs — 114b. Protestant churches in recent years have failed to give their lay leadership adequate training in Christian doctrine. There are now available simple, usable texts for such a course.

The Church Through the Centuries — 131b. The religion of Jesus Christ is transmitted through a fellowship of believers. Anyone preparing to teach his gospel needs a survey of the purpose and history of the Church.

Why I Am a Protestant. If we are to meet the issues of the day, more emphasis than we have had in the immediate past must be put on the meaning of a free religion.

*Planning and Leading Christian Worship — 144a or 144b. The basic nature of this experience is obvious, both for the development of personal religious living and for guiding others into the presence of God.

The Church and Social Action — 133b. " Faith without works is dead." Our prospective workers should understand that discipleship involves the painful task of applying the gospel to the social issues of the day.

At Work for a Christian World — 151a or 151b. The heart of the Christian message is its evangelistic appeal. Christian education emphasizes the fact that the good news is to be shared with all men everywhere. Church leaders should catch the vision of the missionary job ever present in the local community, as well as in the nation and throughout the world.

*The Pupils We Teach — 140a or 140b. The suggestion here is a simple outline study in human psychology, which will serve as a basis for understanding our pupils.

*Ways of Teaching — 141a or 141b. Fundamental principles and techniques in the use of materials and methods would be the content of such a course for beginners. Good teaching is in essence the same at all age levels. Many adaptations could be made as the students observe, do practice teaching in the Sunday school, and report on their experiences.

Since these courses are elementary in nature, they are usually offered on the First Series level. However, there is no objection to doing a more thorough and comprehensive job if the group so desire. No effort has been made to list all the courses apprentice or cadet workers may take. The local church should feel free to offer any experience along this line that will help to meet its needs. Nor is it assumed that all eleven of those mentioned above should be required of every person planning to serve the church. But for an individual totally without training or experience in educational or religious leadership, the five marked with an asterisk would seem to be pretty essential.

Each local church should strive for a leadership at least "two deep" for every post under its supervision. A carefully planned and faithfully administered program of apprentice training is probably the most effective means of reaching this goal. This fact may be illustrated by quoting from a letter from the minister of Christian education, Fourth Presbyterian Church, Chicago 11, Illinois:

"We started a new classification of teachers this fall, which we call associate teachers. Associate teachers are assigned to a class that has a regular full-time teacher. They are subject to the same requirements as our regular staff in the way of attendance at departmental meetings and parent-teacher meetings, and reading books from our church library. . . . They have a minimum attendance requirement of two out of four Sundays. This enables them to observe the work of a competent teacher and to correlate the theoretical knowledge, which they get from our training courses, with the practical know-how of actual class sessions. The plan was started this fall, and we now have associate teachers for approximately forty per cent of our classes. We hope eventually to have associates for all classes in all departments."

Another church, which plans its activities far in advance, has written up a training program for the senior department of its church school. We quote from the leaflet which describes it.[2]

"*Members of the Senior Department of the Church School:* You have come to that period of your Christian education when the church offers you a sixfold program of instruction, activities, and leadership

---

[2] *The Church Program for the Senior Department of the Church School,* Central Presbyterian Church, Lafayette, Indiana.

training, in preparation for a more abundant Christian life and Christian leadership. The Sunday and weekday activities explained in this folder include: (1) Sunday school instruction and worship, (2) participation in the regular church program, (3) a special course in leadership training, (4) weekday activities, (5) ceremonials and rituals, and (6) a summer schedule of conferences and outings. Participation in all these is necessary for a well-rounded development.

"*Leadership:* On each Sunday evening, during the school year, from 5:30 to 9:00 P.M., you are offered special training for Christian leadership. This training may be completed in less than three years. At the completion of your youth leadership training course you will be recognized and honored before the morning congregation on the annual Youth Day Sunday. You will receive a certificate of achievement, a complete notebook of guide sheets, and a modern translation of the Bible.

" The leadership training course for seniors offers a variety of interests and many hours of good fellowship. The study program includes Biblical literature, Church music, hymnody, worship, drama, discussion groups, and special speakers. In the field of recreation many handicrafts, individual sports, group and party games, folk dances and songs are learned.

" Each member of the group may serve on the Four Commissions of (1) worship and study, (2) service, (3) fellowship, and (4) personnel, and have an active voice in the planning of the program. All of the course of study is presented in a regularly scheduled outline for the senior leadership training groups which meet each Sunday evening. Those who take part in this Sunday evening program come to appreciate, not only its opportunities for a complete Christian education, but also an experience of happy Christian fellowship.

" Seniors who complete their leadership training as offered by the church are given opportunities from time to time to be instructors in camps and conferences and to take a special part as leaders in the program of the church.

" If you are a member of the senior department of the church school, you are urged to consider with serious intent this sixfold program which your church offers for your development, and you are invited to make it your own personal program of achievement and advancement for Christ and his Kingdom."

Courses for In-Service Training

A minister who has been teaching leadership training classes in his church for years writes, in part, as follows about his experience:

"Early in my ministry I recognized the fact that the only way for a church to have a really adequate and effective leadership is for that church to train its own leaders. Just sitting back and waiting for leaders to turn up doesn't provide them in the average church. I also recognized that such training is largely the responsibility of the pastor, and is, I believe, one of his major tasks.

"My first pastorate was for fifteen years, and I found an ever increasing joy in sitting down with our leaders, prospective leaders, and other interested folks, and thinking through together this matter of leadership. We tried to give our people three opportunities each year for a standard course or its equivalent. Usually I taught two courses, and one was provided through the community leadership school. This method proved rewarding in the building of leadership, both in numbers and in quality."

From the American Baptist Convention

"Training Leaders for Your Church"[3] is the title of a pamphlet distributed by the American Baptist Publication Society which describes a program of leadership education for local Baptist churches. While designed for a particular denomination, it is suggestive to all, because it has been planned with a definite purpose and is adaptable to a church of any size. The Baptists state that:

The Basic Courses, four in number, are designed to help the leader to secure a foundation in training upon which additional work can be done. In other words, these four courses represent the very minimum level of training to be expected of any leader in the church school. They include (1) the course on the personal religious faith and practice of the leader; (2) a study of the life of Christ; (3) methods of teaching; and (4) a consideration of the total program of Christian education for local Baptist churches, First Series.

The titles of these courses are: (1) **Personal Christian Living.** (2) **The Life of Jesus.** (3) **Introduction to Teaching.** (4) **The Baptist Church School.**

The Advanced Courses, Second Series, have been planned to enable the leader to further his program of training. A background knowledge of the Bible; an understanding of the history and distinctive witness of the Baptists; an appreciation of the challenge and responsibility of the missionary endeavor; and a workable knowledge of the practical aspects of the leader's task are uniquely combined in

[3] Leadership Education Department, Board of Christian Education, American Baptist Convention.

the Advanced Courses. A careful study of these courses will enrich the leader's own life, and greatly enhance his effectiveness as an instrument of God.

The Advanced Courses require a minimum of ten fifty-minute class sessions and an equivalent number of hours spent outside in study and assigned work. In order that the subject may be presented most effectively, however, each course is planned so as to cover twelve fifty-minute sessions.

This venture of the Baptists has met with widespread success through the country, demonstrating that a productive discipline in leadership training is possible at the local church level.

From the Protestant Episcopal Church

Bridging Some Gaps in Our Present Programs of Christian Education is the title of a course provided for use in local churches by the Department of Christian Education of this denomination. It is designed for ten sessions of two hours each. The first three lessons deal with specifications for the new Episcopal curriculum. The other seven are concerned with how to study and use the Bible in home and church. The purposes of the course are clearly stated in the booklet mentioned above, as follows:

" To help rectors who are baffled by the educational program. . . . ' Teaching is not telling ' sums up neatly if negatively a good deal of modern educational philosophy. The seminary training of the average clergyman included practically nothing about educational philosophy and procedure and much emphasis on telling. He desires sincerely to fulfill more ably the teaching as well as the preaching function of his ministry.

" To help parents who desire for their children good Christian training, but feel themselves inadequate to the task, because they realize that they themselves have no intelligent grasp of Christian truth or of the relevance of the Christian gospel to life, and who usually have very hazy ideas of what is meant by Christian nurture.

" To help church school teachers who almost without exception deplore their lack of knowledge and specific training for their task, and who desire sincerely to serve the Master better in this important field of Christian service."

From the Southern Baptist Convention

The Southern Baptists have long emphasized leadership education in the local church through the development of a special program known as " The Baptist Training Union." This is a unique plan for training young and old in the meaning and responsibilities of church membership, with a view to developing people who can assume positions of leadership in the church. The program lives, moves, and has its being in the life of the local congregation. Two manuals outlining the aims, organization, and work of the Union have been written by its General Secretary and Director, Rev. J. E. Lambdin. One is designed for large churches and the other for the small, " nondepartment " church.[4] A condensation taken from Dr. Lambdin's writings in these two booklets, and from personal correspondence, will give us a picture of this tool for developing church leadership.

The Baptist Training Union grew out of the Baptist Young People's Union. This was originally an organization for young people only, seventeen years of age and above. Its success and expansion led to the development of the modern graded Union, which is now the agency for training local church members of all ages. This organization is recognized as an essential part of Christian education in every Baptist church. It is graded to make a place for all church members, and for children below the junior department who are not church members. The aim of the Baptist Training Union is " training in church membership." The word " training " as here used is an educational term. It implies that every church member should be an educated church member, well versed in all the fundamentals of the Christian faith and developed in skill to do church work. Church membership should be a rare privilege and should be held only by those who are children of God through the new birth. To be an active, participating church member one must have Christian intelligence and spiritual skill. These can come only through worship, study, and Christian training. The Training Union offers development in the individual Christian life, development in church life, and development in denominational life. This course of training in church membership is also the finest type of training for Christian living outside one's immediate church experience.

[4] *The Baptist Training Union Manual* and *Building a Church Training Program.*

In the more expanded description of the plan [5] it is made abundantly clear that the Training Union renders a unique service to individual Christian lives and to the church as an institution. The purpose is not only to enrich the lives of individual Christians in the Unions, but also to develop their initiative and whatever powers of leadership they may possess. For instance, the Training Union puts special emphasis on preparation for soulwinning. It gives careful instruction in the meaning and practice of stewardship. But its major contribution to the life of the church as an institution is through recruiting and training of denominational leaders. Dr. Lambdin says that the Training Union has thoroughly justified its existence in this one ministry, regardless of its value in other ways.

Several questions occur to the reader as he analyzes the materials on the Baptist Training Union. Let us pose three of the most important and ask Dr. Lambdin to answer them.

1. What is the relationship of the Union to the Sunday school?

ANSWER: " In our Baptist churches the Sunday school and the Training Union are allies in the total Christian educational program of a church. Each one is set up as an agency of the church and each one is under the control and supervision of the church. Correlation is achieved through the leadership of the pastor and his staff. Neither of these agencies is subordinate to the other. The church itself is a school and each of these great agencies is a department in that school.

" The Training Union is graded and departmentalized along the same lines as the Sunday school, but the units of the organization within the departments are different. In the Training Union we have unions, which are divided into groups and committees. The members of a union operate the organization, and a group in each union presents the program every Sunday evening. This provides one of the opportunities for individual participation.

" The Training Union, in a sense, supplements and extends the work of the Sunday school. It brings help to pastors in keeping churches open on Sunday evenings with a vital, dynamic service. Wherever a Baptist church has a Training Union, it has a Sunday evening service, with preaching following the Training Union."

2. What is the relationship of the Union to the Leadership Education program of the Sunday School Department of the Southern Baptist Convention?

[5] *The Baptist Training Union Manual*, pp. 42–46.

ANSWER: " There is no conflict at all with the specialized training curriculum for Sunday school workers offered by our Sunday School Department. In fact, the instruction we give in the Training Union is splendid preparation for advanced specialization in all phases of Sunday school work in the fields of teaching and administration."

3. *How has the Church responded to the challenge of the Union which demands so much in time and personal sacrifice?*

ANSWER: " I am happy to report that we are making splendid progress in reaching our Baptist church members with the Training Union on Sunday evenings. The enrollment for 1948 is reported officially as more than 1,000,000. We have hundreds of Training Unions, ranging in membership from 500 to 1,000. We have a few with an enrollment going beyond the 1,000 mark. The small rural churches are taking it up in a splendid way. Circulation of our Training Union periodicals reached a grand total in the fourth quarter of 1948 of 1,516,462. The *Adult Union Quarterly* has gone beyond 40,000 and each one of the age group periodicals has a comparable distribution."

Those responsible for Leadership Education in this Union have never been far from the problems of the local church in their thinking and planning. They have designed machinery adaptable to a church of any size, which, if used as directed, seems to produce the leaders that church may need.

Adequate recognition is given for participation and services rendered. One may indeed ask the question as to whether the whole business of awards and credits is overdone. But the reply can always be made that it is better to *recognize* than to *ignore*, provided rewards are conditioned on honest effort. There is nothing in the literature of the Southern Baptists to indicate that the crown is awarded without the cross.

Illustrations presented thus far demonstrate both the interest in and the possibility of offering worth-while training courses in the local church. Let us observe how an experience of this kind may work out in actual practice.

The Grace Presbyterian Church, Council Bluffs, Iowa, has been offering a series of leadership training courses for its workers, usually consisting of six lessons and running through the fall, winter, and spring months. The prospectus is submitted herewith.

PROGRAM OF LEADERSHIP EDUCATION
GRACE PRESBYTERIAN CHURCH
ADULT STUDY COURSES

First Series

Thursday evenings at 7:30 or Sunday afternoons at 3:30

FALL	WINTER	SPRING
October 9 to December 11	February 5 to March 18	April 29 to May 27 (Thurs.)
October 12 to December 14	February 8 to March 21	April 2 to May 30 (Sun.)
GOD'S DEALING WITH MANKIND	GOD'S DEALING WITH MANKIND	GOD'S DEALING WITH MANKIND
Moses — Jeremiah	Samuel — Esther	Literature and Propaganda
OUR PROTES-TANT AND PRESBYTERIAN HERITAGE	THE CHURCH MUST TEACH . . . OR DIE	RECREATIONAL MATERIALS AND METHODS FOR THE CHURCH

Second Series

PAUL LAUNCHES THE NEW TESTAMENT	THE GENERAL LETTERS AND THE JOHN BOOKS	THE GOSPEL OF JESUS CHRIST
THE HISTORY OF CHRISTIAN BELIEFS	PERSONALITY READJUSTMENT PROBLEMS	WHAT HAPPENS WHEN WE WORSHIP

You may register for as many units as you desire. There is no fee. Two courses are offered each class session, one in the Bible and the other in leadership principles and skills.

New material will be presented on Thursday evening and repeated on Sunday afternoon for those who miss on Thursday or who can attend only on Sunday.

Texts for the Bible Courses: The Holy Bible, preferably a modern translation, with good print. The 12 study booklets in the *Know Your Bible Series,* by Roy L. Smith. (These will be available as we need them.)

Text for " The Church Must Teach . . . or Die." Study Guide by the same name.

> *Note:* Two-ring notebook binders will be provided to hold the mimeographed outlines used each week.
> *The Teacher:* The pastor.
> *Please register in advance.*

In presenting this opportunity to his people, the minister of the church makes clear what he has in mind by saying:

" We expect that these courses will be a training school for the teachers of the church school as well as leaders of other organizations in the church. We invite to its membership also all who are interested in learning the Christian way of life and we hope that it will be in some measure helpful to you."

Successful results with leadership training courses in the local church call for planning ahead. This should be the responsibility of the committee on leadership education, in co-operation with the pastor. Wise selection of courses, careful choice of dates, adequate publicity, personal invitations, provision of a comfortable place to meet, above all, a competent instructor — these are among the items that must receive faithful attention if such a program is to achieve its purpose. However, if it has consistent support from the minister and the congregation, it can produce amazing results in the life of the church.

Chapter VII

COMMUNITY LEADERSHIP EDUCATION CLASSES

Community schools of leadership training supplement and reinforce the program of the local church in developing effective workers for Christian education. Such schools reveal our common interests. They give a sense of reality to Protestant co-operation. They encourage a sharing of ideas and problems, which frequently carries over into the continuing experience of those who participate. Above all, they stir enthusiasm and provide skilled instruction guided by high standards of educational achievement.

Two types of community leadership schools are widely prevalent. One is represented by a group of churches from a single denomination. The other is a joint enterprise undertaken on an interdenominational basis. Since most denominations follow the plan of the Division of Christian Education, N. C. C. C., in setting up their community schools, we shall give our primary attention to the interdenominational pattern.

The first step is the appointment of a committee on leadership education responsible to the local council of churches or ministerial association. Membership should be widely representative of denominations and individual churches. On a good committee will be found both ministers and lay leaders. Agencies allied in purpose with the church should also be represented, such as the Y.M.C.A., the Y.W.C.A., the public-school staff, and the Parent-Teacher Association. Those who select this committee would do well to remember the interests of different age groups and other organizations in the church — for instance, the council of church-women and the men of the church. This committee must have a broad base, if its work is to continue without interruption when some key leader departs from the community.

Responsibility of the committee on leadership education should center in policy-making and securing enthusiastic community support. Details can well be left to smaller subcommittees dealing with such matters as promotion and publicity, budget and finances, curriculum and faculty, and other problems as they arise. Great care should be exercised in the choice of people who will serve as chairmen of these subcommittees. The success or failure of the project will depend largely upon their wisdom and energy.

The Division of Christian Education, N. C. C. C., has outlined carefully steps to be taken in setting up a successful community leadership training school. Suggestions that follow are based upon its long and fruitful experience in this field.[1]

Prerequisites of Success

1. Thorough long-time planning.

2. Good teaching which meets the real needs of persons, both for their own enrichment and in their particular tasks.

3. Effective promotion, not only of the project but of the larger purpose, so that there will be transfer from the school to the particular churches.

4. High morale; good fellowship and joyful participation.

5. A deep spiritual purpose and devotional tone which makes the teaching-learning experience minister to the religious life of the students.

6. Proper recognition of attainment; public awarding of course cards and fitting recognition in the local church of the workers' efforts to improve their contribution.

7. Adequate follow-up — many a teacher has been discouraged when the inspiration and new ideas he received in leadership enterprises found no way of expression or recognition back in his own church.

8. Opportunities for continued help to those with a newly awakened sense of need.

[1] *A Manual for Deans.*

Make a Survey of Present Opportunities and Prospective Needs

It is important to know what is now being done for leadership education in the community. This ought to be a thorough inventory, seeking answers to questions such as these:

1. What general denominational programs, if any, are in progress or immediately contemplated? If there is a community school of leadership education, how long has it been in existence?

2. What local church training is being done, i.e., classes, workers' conferences, coaching, etc.?

3. How may the work that can be done on the community basis augment and supplement and stimulate what is being done by individual churches or by denominations, and not seem to be an " extra " or in competition?

4. What present community educational activities and facilities may contribute training opportunities for church workers, such as extension courses, Y.M.C.A. classes, group work training projects, etc.?

5. Is there any sense of need on the part of the churches, or a sufficient sense of need to make a good beginning?

6. If not, how can it be motivated? If so, what needs seem to be felt?

7. How well can the school be set up and prompted to catch a ready response, because it seems to be just *what the churches have been looking for?*

8. What leaders and equipment are available?

It is advisable to plan the school within the larger framework of leadership education in the community. Admittedly a community school of one, two, or even three terms is an important part, *but only a part,* of an adequate program. Aim always at a co-ordinated effort, continuous and productive of lasting results, building on what has gone before.

Too much stress is often placed on one outstanding success, to the neglect of subsequent opportunities and changing conditions. The steady, unspectacular effort gathers cumulative power as it develops, thus convincing both workers and churches of the values in the training experience.

Carefully Select and Train Key Workers

The ultimate success, or one might better say the continued growth, of leadership education projects in the community will depend upon the excellence of the leadership. Mediocre teaching and group work will soon defeat the best promotion. While some professional or expert leadership is a great asset in the school, indigenous leaders are often available who can do a grand job. As far as possible, the leaders ought to be close to the persons in the school — aware of their problems, of their outlook, of their religious backgrounds, and the attitudes of their churches. Good leadership must be in dead earnest, inspired, consecrated, willing to work hard, and *growing all the time*. These steps should be followed in selecting and training workers:

1. Select the best leaders that the budget will permit and give them plenty of time to prepare.

2. Help them to get ready by: interpreting carefully the job to be done, the aims of the school, the needs you hope to meet, the sort of help the churches want.

3. Schedule faculty meetings in advance, during the school and after, for evaluation and future planning.

4. Send some key persons, who have capacity for creative teaching, to summer schools and conferences, with the idea of giving them wider service as they develop.

5. Plan a coaching conference for the instructors of leadership courses. Local public-school teachers and others may help them to prepare. Perhaps a field worker can be brought in to coach the faculty.

Ministers can and should do a great deal of teaching in leadership schools. However, the quality of their service varies tremendously. One temptation of busy ministers is inadequate preparation, perhaps hurried at the last minute, or piecemeal after the course is under way. Another is to deliver a series of lectures or to sermonize on the theme of the course. This may be most interesting, but makes little contribution to a worker's effectiveness back on the job in his own church.

The chief aim is to get good teachers wherever they may be

found. If a pastor fits this pattern, he should be encouraged. Perhaps brother ministers might help him with other community duties. At least, he should be recognized as giving a valuable service to the cause of Christian education. Division of responsibility could be developed. One pastor might become an " expert " in counseling, another in youth work, another in worship, another in how to study and teach the Bible. Sharing in such informal " staff arrangement" would greatly enhance the work of each. Many pastors would profit from taking special classes in the art of teaching and supervision, such as " The Minister as Christian Educator "; " Ways of Teaching "; " How to Supervise Education in the Local Church."

Securing " headliners " from the outside may or may not prove to be a profitable investment. The right person, who can really do a good job, will add prestige to the school and bring great help to those who take his work. But there are pitfalls in simply looking for a name to help to " put the school over." If we sell big names instead of purpose, we overshadow the patient, and often more important, work of local teachers. We have always to look in each succeeding school for a bigger name as a drawing card. Often we fail to develop local talent sufficiently. In the long run, the same amount of time and money spent in developing local leaders pays off much better.

Frequently excellent instructors may be found among public-school people who are devoted Christians and faithful church workers. They generally prepare carefully; their reputation in the community as educators means something to them.

Plan for the years ahead. There are in most communities modest persons with a natural talent for helping others to grow while they grow themselves. Cultivate these prospects. Send them to conferences or summer schools. Most communities can develop in a few years a corps of leaders well trained in guiding other persons. There are now in this country many people who themselves only a short while ago were quietly doing a good job in their own local church schools, but who now are much in demand for a wide variety of enterprises in leadership training. *Some such persons of potential power are in your community!*

Promote Vigorously

It is especially important in community schools that there be a strong promotion program. Write to the Division of Christian Education, N. C. C. C., for information regarding its recently devised promotional helps, which are proving their worth wherever they have been used, namely: the poster, postcard, and bulletin series for advertising community leadership training schools; and the specific and practical suggestions in *Publicity Strategy*, which has just come from the press. The following procedures contribute to good promotion:

1. Enlist the ministers and keep them interested. Leadership education needs strong lay support, but the pastor is a key leader. Plans for this work rarely succeed in churches where the minister is indifferent.

2. Secure the participation of church school superintendents and directors of religious education, in planning, in promotion, and in the work of the school.

3. Set dates well in advance, after conferring with those in authority. See that these dates get into the little engagement books of ministers, superintendents, and others. Do not let the time for the community school be squeezed in as an extra after most other dates are chosen.

4. See that a live contact is made with each church. If the pastor does not seem vitally interested, drive through to lay leaders. Some communities appoint a contact person for each church.

5. Secure " official " church endorsement if possible. Payment of registration fees out of church budgets is not only good finance but excellent promotion.

6. Send " minute men " to individual churches to promote the leadership school.

7. Get the announcement of the school on church bulletins. Someone may be assigned to handle this feature only — it takes persistent checking.

8. Try advance registration. It takes effort. It is often disappointing, but it has good promotion value.

9. Use newspapers and radio stations. Several notices can be managed if the stories differ. Give titles and aims of specific courses. Play up features such as outstanding faculty members and special periods which are planned.

10. Select an attractive name for the school. These have been used and are suggestive:

CHRISTIAN SERVICE TRAINING SCHOOL

INSTITUTE OF CHRISTIAN SERVICE

CHRISTIAN LEADERSHIP SCHOOL

LIFE AND LEADERSHIP SCHOOL

SCHOOL IN CHRISTIAN LIVING

CHURCH WORKERS' INSTITUTE

SCHOOL OF RELIGION

11. Sell the general idea of better preparation as you promote a particular training project. The school is not an end but a means.

Provide Adequate Financial Support

Expenses of a leadership school can be kept to a minimum. Printing, postage, and accreditation fees are customary items in the budget. Sometimes the church where the school is held makes a small charge for light and heat and janitor service. Instructors should also be furnished their textbooks free of charge. However, most schools, especially in smaller communities, do not pay an honorarium to the instructors. Travel costs should be met, particularly for faculty members who come from out of town. Sometimes it is necessary to pay an honorarium in order to get the person who is desired for a particular task. Policies in these matters vary considerably. The local churches should be a controlling factor in what is finally agreed upon.

Schools are often financed through registration fees. A more solid foundation is provided, however, if the budget is underwritten by the churches in the community. Sometimes the churches are asked to pay a registration fee at so much per person up to a certain maximum, after which as many persons may be sent as can be enrolled. If the expense of the school is distributed among the churches, it is necessary to find an equitable basis on which to share the financial burden.

Things to Remember

In beginning community leadership training, it is highly important really to help people at the point of their needs. Too often the approach is over their heads; while in itself excellent and interesting, what they receive seems remote from their current problems in their own church schools. *We must know the conditions under which they work; the curriculum materials they use; their general background and attitudes.*

" Start where they are." Develop the fullest possible participation from the outset. Spraying people with words does not produce notable results in improved practice.

Every school should provide a large amount of opportunity for dealing with individual problems. It is often possible to have some extra counselors for personal interviews as well as instructors for the classes.

Remember that beginning teachers or teachers with no formal training often need help most in very elemental but difficult matters, i.e., understanding the curriculum they are using, its aims, how it is planned, etc.; how to plan a class session; how to start and end a class session; how to prepare for a project and initiate it; how to get pupil participation; how to use maps, Bible dictionaries, and other helps.

It would be a great thing in most communities if the pastors would go to school with their workers. It would set a good example. They would know what their workers are getting and whether it suits their needs. They would know how to follow up back on the job in the local church. They could build on the beginning that the school has made in improving the study habits and techniques of its workers.

Make Use of the Following Resources

Denominational Board of Christian Education: Each denomination represented by a co-operating church might be asked to send literature that would help the planning committee. Denominations have special emphases from time to time. Knowledge of these and use when possible would tend to tie these emphases into an intelligible pattern.

Field Men of Denominational Boards of Christian Education:
There is generally a field worker of one of the co-operating denominations who is available to meet with the committee to help
to plan, if his services are requested early so that he can work a
call into his schedule.

State Councils of Churches and Religious Education: State and
local councils of churches provide immediate help and supervision to leadership schools serving the groups which they represent.

The Division of Christian Education, N. C. C. C.: Leaders'
guides are available for most of the courses listed in the following bulletins:

> Bulletin 501 . . *First Series Courses of the Standard Leader-
> ship Curriculum.*
>
> Bulletin 502 . . *Second Series Courses of the Standard Leader-
> ship Curriculum.*
>
> Bulletin 507 . . *And Gladly Serve* — A Program for Enlisting
> and Developing Church
> Workers.

A Manual for Deans.

At Your Best (leaflet setting forth the requirements for Certificates of Progress).

The Division of Christian Education is also ready at any time
to offer advice and assistance to a local group regarding the organization and accreditation of leadership training schools.

Following are several illustrations of creative projects in community programs of leadership education taken from different
sections of the country.

Massachusetts — The Massachusetts Council of Churches has developed a plan of training teachers in laboratory schools in the local community. Three such laboratory schools have been conducted. In each
of these schools the laboratory sessions were held during the regular
Sunday school period, with an additional session of an hour or more
each week for evaluation, discussion, and planning. The teachers-in-
training did one to two hours of assigned reading each week in a
standard text. In each of these schools the teachers enrolled have been

high in their praise of the plan as a practical means for learning how to teach more effectively. The enrollment and attendance on the part of these teachers both on Sunday morning and at the week-night sessions clearly established the fact that volunteer lay workers can be enrolled for this more thorough type of training, and the further fact that in cases where they already have responsibilities in their own Sunday schools they can be released for this training by the use of substitutes.

North Carolina — Queens College, Charlotte, North Carolina, has co-operated for several years with the churches of the city in promoting and staffing an interdenominational leadership training program for the entire community. Usually three schools have been held each year. Following is a brief description of how this project was organized and projected. It is taken from a letter written by the president of the college to interested persons in the community:

" A group of Charlotte churches, on an interdenominational basis, are co-operating with Queens College in adding a professor of religious education to the faculty of the college. The duties of this professor will be as follows:

" 1. Under her direction, there will develop in Charlotte an interdenominational teacher training program for all Sunday school workers. The personnel resources for such a program will be the faculty of Queens College, the directors of religious education in the local churches of Charlotte, the pastors of these churches, and, perhaps, from time to time, teachers from outside the local community. It will be a continuous program of religious education, with courses planned over a period of years, and these courses given in a series throughout the year, meeting either once or twice a week in the evening. All Sunday school workers of the city, regardless of denomination, will have the privilege of sharing in these training courses.

" 2. The professor of religious education at Queens College will seek to have each student of the college find her place in some church of the community, where she will be at home, and also where she will participate in the work of the church. We shall hope that the young women who attend Queens College will, during their college years, become so interested in the work of the church that in the communities where later they will reside they will become leaders for the church. We believe that in the field of church work a program may be developed of laboratory experience in church work, corresponding to the practice teaching program in the field of education.

" 3. This teacher at the college will also be an addition to the department of religion and philosophy. It has been suggested that a course be given for our college students on the history of the Ecumenical Church. This teacher should not have too heavy a teaching load in the college, so that much of her time might be given to her community work. She probably would not teach more than two courses in the department of religion and philosophy.

" 4. The suggestion has been made by which the college may participate more effectively, through this program, in assisting the churches in daily vacation Bible schools, mission work, etc. It would be our hope that students of Queens College would be active, both in Charlotte and, in the summer, elsewhere, in promoting the work of the church.

" 5. We believe that through such an effort, more of our young women will be encouraged to give themselves definitely to the work of the Church by taking postgraduate work to prepare themselves to be Bible teachers, directors of religious education, and missionaries."

The plan was successfully consummated and has been in operation for several years. Its chief purpose, namely, " to lift the quality of Christian teaching in the community," has been realized in gratifying measure.

Ohio — We have here a less ambitious projection of leadership education, but one which has made a splendid contribution to the community in which it has been operating. The program of one winter school is reproduced in full as a sample of what can be done when a state and county work together for leadership education. Note that the careful selection of faculty members involves public-school people, college professors, directors of religious education, and ministers of local churches.

CHRISTIAN LEADERSHIP TRAINING SCHOOL

FOR

BETTER PREPARED TEACHERS AND LEADERS IN THE CHURCH SCHOOL

at

The First Methodist Church
227 Tuscarawas Street, West Canton, Ohio

on

Six Tuesday Evenings, 7:30 to 9:30 O'clock

January 10	January 31
January 17	February 7
January 24	February 14

Sponsored by:

CHRISTIAN EDUCATION COMMITTEE

of the

CANTON–STARK COUNTY MINISTERS' ASSOCIATION

THE SECOND SERIES OF THE STANDARD LEADERSHIP CURRICULUM
TO BE OFFERED BY THE SCHOOL

120b How the Bible Came to Be: A course dealing with such questions as how different types of literature, such as poetry, history, biography, came to be written; why the need for stories of Jesus' life caused certain persons to write the Gospels; and how the growth of the early Christian churches caused the letters of the New Testament to be written.

Instructor: Dr. James Anderson, Professor of Bible and Religious Education, The College of Wooster.

Textbook: *How Came the Bible?* by Edgar J. Goodspeed.

124b Jesus and His Teachings: The purpose of this course is to lead to an increased acquaintance with the main emphasis made by Jesus in his teachings, to a better understanding of the meaning of his teaching for personal and social living today, and to a more active part in carrying his teachings into effect.

Instructor: Rev. Edgar A. Walker, Ph.D., General Presbyter, the Presbyterian Church, U. S. A.

Textbook: *The Message of Jesus,* by B. H. Branscomb.

140b Understanding Our Pupils: What makes persons act as they do? What are persons of various age groups interested in? How and why do persons differ? What are the best ways of finding out about the background, experience, prejudices, interests of persons, and the causes of their actions and attitudes? Why did Jesus have such high respect for personality? The course includes a consideration of major human wishes or urges, heredity and environment, physical growth, emotional and social adjustments, and the significance of religion for persons of all ages.

Instructor: Mr. Melvin Bixler, Assistant Superintendent, Stark County Board of Education.

Textbook: *A Growing Person,* by F. C. McLester.

141b Ways of Teaching: The values of lecturing, of telling a story, of discussion, of drama, and of service for others are considered in this course as the students try to learn how to use the best ways of teaching. How to plan for the class session, how to use the Bible, the quarterly, or the textbook, may be studied. How to appeal to the interests of the pupils one is teaching and how to guide their interests into worth-while enterprises are major problems of the course.

Instructor: Mr. Dwight Flohr, Superintendent, Grade School, North Industry.

Textbook: *New Trails for the Christian Teacher,* by R. S. Smith.

216b The Use of the Bible with Children: This course is planned to meet the needs of all departmental leaders in the children's division, beginning with the nursery department. It is intended to help workers with children to examine the purposes and principles as well as effective ways of using the Bible with children.

Instructor: Miss Elizabeth Hartman, Director of Religious Education, First Methodist Church, Cuyahoga Falls, Ohio.

Textbook: *The Use of the Bible with Children,* by E. L. Smither.

312b   The Church's Program for Youth: This course is planned for seniors, young people, and adult leaders of intermediates, seniors, and young people. What goals to have and how to determine them, what steps to take in building a youth program, what leaders to have and what their functions should be, what materials to use, the place of youth in the work of the church, and what records to keep, are some of the questions for consideration in this course.

Instructor: Rev. Orville W. Briner, Associate Minister, First Presbyterian Church, Canton, Ohio.

Textbook: *Youth Work in the Church,* by Nevin C. Harner.

Learn with others in an accredited Leadership Training School under the leadership of well-qualified instructors.

All active church school workers, and especially prospective workers of senior high school age or older, are eligible to enroll.

Register for only one course. A registration fee of $1.00 is required for each student.

Regular attendance is necessary to be eligible for credit toward Certificates of Progress.

Textbooks for each course will be on sale at the opening session.

Appoint a representative in your church to enlist and enroll students. A supply of bulletins and enrollment cards will be furnished by the publicity committee.

School Organization

BOARD CHAIRMAN: Rev. Arthur Harsh.

BOARD SECRETARY: Miss Helen Worthman.

FACULTY AND CURRICULUM COMMITTEE: Mr. Warren J. Carter, Chairman; Rev. Orville W. Briner, Mr. C. W. Studer.

PUBLICITY COMMITTEE: Mr. L. West Shea, Chairman; Mr. C. E. Lowe, Mr. C. J. Hunt, Mr. Howard H. Eutzly.

REGISTRATION: Mr. L. D. Chenot, Registrar; Mr. Melvin Moncrief, Mrs. Ray D. Bender.

FINANCE COMMITTEE: Mr. M. G. Watts, Chairman; Mr. Roy Luke, Treasurer; Mr. Charles Stewart, Mr. Donald Bechtel.

DEAN: Mr. Paul G. Schneider, 352 Dryden Avenue, N.W., Canton, Ohio. Telephone, 2-2816.

Kindly address communications and inquiries concerning the school to the dean.

Wyoming — The new technique of *Group Dynamics* was used in the Adult Conference at Story, Wyoming, during the summer of 1950. This is a fresh approach to group leadership, developed out of research directed by Kurt Lewin at the University of Iowa and his colaborers at the University of Michigan. The chief conclusion of all the studies thus far made is that the most productive type of leadership is a function of the group itself, rather than the responsibility of any single individual.

Organization of the group involves selection of a chairman, a recorder or secretary, and a group observer. The chairman is supposed to be a thoroughly democratic leader, who neither dominates the group nor allows it merely to drift. The recorder keeps accurate notes of the major opinions expressed and on decisions reached. The observer, from time to time, at the request of the group, summarizes progress, sharpens issues, and points out elements of failure. He keeps a close watch on how the group operates and helps it to look at its procedures.

The chairman, as a member of the group, takes the initiative at the beginning to help in selecting objectives, in organizing for business, and in agreeing upon procedures of operation. Knowles reminds us, however, that the group is conceived as an independent, self-directing organism. Hence, we refer to " leadership functions " and " a leadership team," rather than " a leader." [2]

The group discovers its own problems and devotes all its time to their solution. Final decisions are its exclusive responsibility. With the help of the observer, the group evaluates its procedures in order to improve the thinking process. It utilizes the resources of its members and accepts the emotional as well as the intellectual contribution of each person. If occasion requires it, an outside specialist may be asked to supply needed information. Groups of this kind are constantly trying out their ideas in life situations.

Additional information about this interesting method of developing group leadership may be secured from the following sources:

1. *Group Dynamics and Education,* by Leland P. Bradford, National Education Association, Washington, D. C.

2. *Two Lessons of Group Dynamics.* Educational Trends Sup-

[2] *Informal Adult Education,* by M. S. Knowles, pp. 63, 64. Association Press.

plement. Educator's Washington Dispatch.

3. *Group Self-analysis of Productivity in the Work Conference*, by Ronald Lippitt. Research Center for Group Dynamics, Massachusetts Institute of Technology.

4. *Human Relations.* Quarterly of the Research Center for Group Dynamics, Ann Arbor, Michigan.

Further study of these new and fascinating developments of the discussion method in the training of leaders is suggested, since nothing more than a brief introduction can be offered here. There is an excellent bibliography at the end of *Informal Adult Education,* to which we have referred.

CHAPTER VIII

TRAINING FOR OUTREACH

The first and most important objective of Christian education is to bring boys and girls, men and women, into a saving relationship with Jesus Christ. Dr. Munro has called our attention to the fact that the early Sunday school movement was intensely evangelistic. The chief aim of Bible teaching was the conversion of the pupil. Sunday school leaders and great evangelists were close friends and co-workers. Dwight L. Moody frequently addressed Sunday school gatherings, with striking response to his call for commitment.[1]

Evangelism techniques vary from one period to another. But Christian education has always been the most successful means of increasing church membership. Conservative estimates indicate that at least 65 per cent of those who unite with the church come through the Sunday school. Most of the others have at some time been taught the simple truths of the gospel. Hence, while the methods of educational evangelism today may differ from those in use a generation ago, the Methodists are right when they tell us that:

" There is no conflict between the work of evangelism and the work of Christian education. A program of Christian education that is not evangelistic in its aim and purpose is not Christian. On the other hand, a program of evangelism that does not involve the educational process is temporary and unsatisfactory." [2]

The church school, along with the other organizations of the church, assumes a duty in evangelism which it can never escape.

[1] *Fellowship Evangelism*, by H. C. Munro, p. 3.
[2] *Teaching for a Verdict*, p. 10. Methodist Board of Education.

It must always be concerned with its missionary or outreach obligation, if it is to remain true to its Christian purpose. Consequently, we find the Protestant denominations in recent years revising their approach to this problem in the local church. Presently, the most ambitious program of educational evangelism is the co-operative venture that carries the title " National Christian Teaching Mission." This is an interdenominational enterprise sponsored by the National Council of Churches. Many of the individual communions have also developed excellent plans of evangelistic outreach, adapted to the aims and materials of their educational program. For example, the subtitle of the booklet put out by the Methodists, to which reference was made above, is " Evangelism in the Church School." The Presbyterians have their " Mission to Teachers "; the Baptists, their " Church School Enlargement Program." The United Lutherans have achieved gratifying success with their " Sunday School Enlistment Demonstration," and one of the best programs of educational evangelism is put on by the Evangelical and United Brethren Church.

All these plans have a twofold purpose, namely, reaching the unchurched through the various classes and organizations of the congregation, with a steady improvement of the church's educational offerings. Common features of all these programs are:

1. Development of a prospect list by means of a community survey or religious census, and through the use of other information made available to the local church.

2. Visitation in the homes of the prospects with skillful invitation and follow-up for enlistment.

3. More thorough preparation for church membership.

4. Self-study and evaluation of the church's Christian education program, with suggestions for advancement.

5. Training of leaders in the techniques of educational evangelism as well as how to hold new members of the organizations once they are secured.

Major Objectives in Training for Outreach

1. To stimulate in the members of the staff a sense of responsibility to win boys and girls and men and women to Jesus Christ.

2. To deepen and enrich the spiritual life of all who participate in the enterprise.

3. To assist teachers and other leaders in finding materials and developing techniques required to accomplish this within the compass of the work of their specific age groups.

4. To help workers to interpret and teach the meaning of churchmanship to all who commit themselves to Christ.

5. To create in pupils and teachers alike a concern for the un-reached in the community — a concern that will lead to definite action.

Suggested Steps in Procedure

It is desirable to have a preliminary conference and examination of the local situation by the pastor and church officers. This should include, not only the official board or boards of the church, but also the group clothed with responsibility for the church's program of Christian education, the director of Christian education if there is one, and the chairman of the committee on evangelism. The purpose of this first step is to secure the intelligent support of the church's official leaders, so that the church school workers may be assured of their interest and co-operation in the plan.

The most important task of this top-level corps of the church's leadership is what Dr. Munro calls a self-study [3] to discover what is being done along the line of educational evangelism at the present time, the resources available for such a program, and whether the work of the church school is good enough to hold new prospects and develop them into Christian disciples. Answers to questions such as the following should be sought:

1. What proportion of our members who come in on confession of faith have been members of the church school? Has the proportion been growing or declining in recent years?

2. What proportion of our pupils come from unchurched homes? How does the population trend in the community compare with the enrollment trend in the church school?

3. About how many children and youth in the community are

[3] *Your Evangelistic Potential*, by H. C. Munro, p. 1.

unreached by any church or Sunday school?

4. How many people during the last twenty-five years have gone from this church into professional Christian service?

5. Are absentees from the sessions of the church school carefully followed up each week?

6. Is there genuine concern for persons in the various organizations of the church?

7. Does the class, department, or group have a responsibility list of persons eligible for membership, who there is reason to believe might be more readily brought into this church than any other?

8. Is a persistent approach made to every person on the responsibility list through fellowship visits and invitations to join the group?

9. What proportion of the parents participate in the life and program of the church by regular attendance and work in one or more organizations?

10. What definite plan or program is under way for winning parents, who are now indifferent, into active participation in the life of the church?

11. Does your church provide for persons of all ages to plan and work and play together in its recreational and fellowship activities as well as the more spiritual undertakings of the congregation?

12. What provision is made in the church for developing the spiritual life of its workers and training them to do a more effective job in their respective capacities? Workers' conferences? Local church training schools? Attendance at summer schools?

13. Is there a Decision Day in your church?

14. How are young and old who join the church trained in the duties and privileges of church membership?

The United Lutherans have a score card entitled " Projects for Achievement " which might be helpful in making this survey. A part of it is given herewith as a sample. It is designed primarily for appraising the work of the Sunday church school. Each project is to be scored on the basis of (a) 40 points, (b) and (c) 30 points each. About each statement ask, " Is this being done? " If the answer is, " Yes, perfectly," take full credit. If the answer is, " No, not at all," score zero. If the answer lies between, mark a score that represents actual conditions, as nearly as you can estimate. On the results of the evaluation, projects will suggest themselves for improvement.

Projects for Achievement

General

SCORE

1. Help to nurture Christian homes by promoting the nursery roll and packet, and the home department.

2. Make the school an integral part of the church's educational program, e.g., through a parish education committee or cabinet.

3. Observe the " Calendar of Causes," with special emphasis upon education endeavors of the synod and the parish school board.

The Bible

1. Supply all the church homes regularly with devotional booklets.

2. Make provision for every family to have a readable copy of the Bible.

3. Encourage pupils and teachers to bring their Bibles to school, and provide readable copies for those who do not do so.

Study

1. Use a variety of teaching methods in classroom instruction.

2. Make provision for pupil participation in classroom activities, and secure home study by pupils and teachers.

3. Provide (according to Lutheran charts) pupils' literature for pupils and teachers, and teachers' guides for teachers in all the teaching agencies of the congregation.

Organization and Administration

1. Adopt a constitution that recognizes the pastor as spiritual head of the school, and hold monthly workers' conferences.

2. Hold sessions *every* Sunday totaling 60–75 minutes each and allowing for brief worship (under 15 minutes),

announcements, etc. (under 5 minutes), and the rest for classroom activities.

3. Keep accurate records of finances, enrollment, attendance, significant events, etc., and make periodic reports in bulletins, and to the church council and congregation.

Leaders

1. Promote the regular preparedness, punctuality, and attendance of the staff, having substitute leaders for all positions.

2. Devise a working plan for continually discovering and enlisting leaders, selecting them on the basis of their consecration, understanding, skill, and personal appeal.

3. Make it possible for all leaders to read *The Parish School*, take one or more courses in leadership education each year, and attend camps, conferences, and conventions for Christian workers.

When understanding and support of the plan on the part of the church's official leaders have been secured, a conference of those leaders with all the church school workers and heads of other organizations is desirable. This meeting should be the beginning of a new and more intimate fellowship in prayer and planning among church officers and volunteer leaders, a fellowship to be continued and strengthened in the series of pastor-teacher conferences outlined below.

This group might come together for the first time with a fellowship supper, followed by a brief inspirational address stressing evangelism as the essential task of the church, the responsibility of teachers and other guides to lead their pupils toward personal acceptance of Christ, the necessity of reaching the homes, and the spiritual equipment required. The program should include a presentation of the local situation as revealed in the earlier meeting. Plenty of time should be allowed for clear explanation and for discussion and questions. The group will probably concur with the pastor and church officers in the approval of the plan and will agree to co-operate in it. The pastor should then announce the series of study periods with the teachers and other leaders, which is the third step in the program. A service of prayer and dedication might well conclude the meeting.

The heart of this preparatory experience is to be found in the training sessions of the church officers, church school workers, and heads of all other organizations. There is a threefold purpose for these conferences: first, deepening the spiritual life of those who participate; second, increasing their evangelistic zeal; third, coaching them in wise and effective procedure for achieving the ends of educational evangelism.

Each church will decide in accordance with its particular situation how many of these study periods should be held and what the time schedule should be. It is suggested that a minimum of five or six conferences will be needed, with about an hour and a half allowed for each one. Every pastor will covet an opportunity for this service to key leaders in his church school program because of its extremely significant and far-reaching possibilities.

Building a Prospect List

Have members of the group offer as many suggestions as they can as to how this ought to be done. The following avenues of approach have been found successful:

1. Compare the church membership roll with the roll of the church school and all other organizations (to discover the unchurched, who are now or have been associated in some way with this particular congregation).

2. Examine vacation and weekday church school records.

3. Keep a continuous record of marriages and births.

4. Follow up visitors who have recently moved into the community.

5. Ask for permission to use the lists of religious preferences of pupils gathered by some public schools.

6. Appoint block watchers, van spotters for newcomers. Use real-estate agency lists. Talk with delivery men and meter readers. Some electric and gas companies will keep you informed of new families.

7. Visit city and county institutions, orphanages, homes for old people, hospitals, prisons, colleges. Spot new communities and those remote from churches.

8. If you co-operate in an interdenominational religious census,

be sure to secure your share of the prospect cards and follow them up.

9. Arrange and carry out a community survey.

Every Home Visitation

The plan for an annual visitation of all homes in the church's natural parish is familiar. There is always the need to interest parents and bring them under the influence of evangelistic teaching. The problem of millions of youth and adults unreached by any church school has had much attention and discussion, but there must be very much more active and persistent effort to locate and interest the unchurched persons in our communities than has been undertaken thus far, except in rather rare instances. A local church visitation should follow these steps:

1. Appoint a committee to take charge.
2. Set the visitation date.
3. Obtain the necessary supplies.
4. Keep the congregation well informed of developments.
5. Enlist as many callers as possible.
6. Map the districts to be visited.
7. Arrange specific assignments.
8. Hold an instruction meeting.
9. Make the visitation.

Calling on the Prospect

1. *When to call.* It is not always possible to know the most convenient time when making the first call. This might vary with the type of community. After the first call there should be information on file that will help the caller in choosing the best time for making subsequent calls. In calling on children it is often best to select a time when both parents are apt to be home.

2. *How to gain an entrance into the home.* Some such statement as, "We are from the Brookside Methodist Church, and have come to make a friendly call," will in most cases gain an entrance, especially in the homes where a pastoral call has already been made. Sometimes it is necessary to go a step farther and add: "We understand that you have a boy of junior age who is

not attending Sunday school. We would like to come in and tell you about our school."

3. *Purpose of the call.* The caller is going to call on a definite person, either to persuade him to become a member of the church school or, in the case of an absentee, to persuade him to return and take his place in the church school. The caller should be informed as to what information is on file concerning the one on whom he is to call and plan his visit accordingly.

4. *When to leave.* Calls should never be prolonged. If the smell of food is in the air, the caller will probably find the hostess sitting on the edge of her chair with visions of a spoiled dinner. Perhaps members of the family are working at irregular hours. The caller should realize that it is best not to linger. The attitude of the hostess often reveals other reasons why the call should not be prolonged. A friendly greeting, a statement of the purposes of the call, discovering a point of mutual interest, a cordial invitation to attend the school, will leave the impression that they are wanted in the school and the caller will be welcomed for another visit.

5. *Additional church information needed:*

The church program. The caller should be familiar with all the scheduled meetings of the church, and their purpose. A stranger is likely to ask questions because he wants to know.

The various church activities. Often an activity that appeals to a mother will lead her to come and bring her child.

What the school offers for each age group. While the call may be in the interest of a child or a particular-age person, there may be other members of the family who will want to know whether or not there is a place for them.

6. *Reporting all calls.* A report of every call should be made on the form provided. This report should be in the hands of the chairman of the follow-up committee within forty-eight hours after the making of the call. The report should include when the call was made, whether or not the prospect was at home, interest manifested. It would be well to record the names of other members of the family who might be interested.

Source Materials for Training in Evangelistic Teaching Activities

Evangelism of Children. Division of Christian Education, N. C. C. C.

Teaching for a Verdict. The Methodist Church.

Guiding Boys and Girls to Christ and *Reaching Others for Christ.* Presbyterian Church, U. S. A.

Fellowship Evangelism, by H. C. Munro.

Sunday School Evangelism and *Catechetical Evangelism.* Evangelical and United Brethren Church.

Teaching for a Verdict has excellent suggestions about methods of evangelism with children:

"Teachers of children should achieve two results in their work: (1) To make their week by week teaching truly evangelistic in aim and content. (2) To teach in such a way that each pupil will make a definite decision for Christ and church membership. This will usually be some time during the pupil's junior or intermediate year.

"Few persons, if any, have ever been converted to the Christian religion without first being taught the simple truths of the gospel. There is a sense therefore in which each lesson taught, each time of worship with children, each weekday activity engaged in is evangelistic. As a teacher helps the child to have an understanding of God, of Jesus, of the Bible, of what it means to be a Christian, that teacher is doing the work of evangelism. It will be recalled that Jesus grew in wisdom, in stature, and in favor with God and man. He *grew.* In this sense evangelism is a continuous process and a good teacher is a real evangelist.

"The child should be taught in such a way that he comes normally and naturally to the time of decision. There is no one time or place for this decision. It may come in the classroom, or as the child walks with his teacher along some quiet way, or as he engages in worship in his department, or as he lives with Christian parents in the family circle. It may come on some special day which has been set apart by the pastor as a time of decision. On Decision Day, along with the other boys and girls, what is more normal and natural than for a child who has been learning of Jesus and who, like all the rest of us, is greatly influenced by the example of his fellows, to declare his love for Jesus and his desire to serve him always?

"A word of caution is needed, however. We must be sure that such a decision is a real decision on the part of each boy and girl. We must avoid the danger of leading boys and girls, under the stress of emotional appeals and a mass movement, to make a decision which is not based upon real conviction. This means that the work of teaching must have been carefully done. It also means that the pastor and the department superintendents must use great care in planning for and conducting the service on Decision Day. We should not, however, allow our fears to govern us. Just because there is a danger that some children may join the church who have not had an experience of God, some pastors and teachers never attempt to lead children to make a decision at all. This is the worst sort of heresy. It is a lack of faith in the power of the Holy Spirit and in the ability of the human spirit to know when God speaks to the soul."

In like manner, the good teacher or organization leader will present the claims of Christ to youth and adults upon every appropriate occasion. Christian young people and older people should also be enlisted to present this appeal throughout the entire community.

Co-operation with the Pastor in Preparation for Church Membership

At this point the group should undertake a brief review of the church's teaching, organization, and discipline. At least two of the five or six sessions will be necessary for this purpose.

Integration of Those Won to Christ Into the Total Program of the Church

Conservation of church membership is a major problem of Protestant denominations. Every person, young or old, who commits his life to Christian discipleship should be given a job in the church. This calls for careful co-operative planning to discover talents, uncover opportunities for service, and match the two. Helpful suggestions are to be found in the publications of the National Christian Teaching Mission, 206 S. Michigan Avenue, Chicago 4, Illinois, and the series of pamphlets on "New Member Care" put out by the Department of Evangelism, Presbyterian Church, U. S. A., 156 Fifth Avenue, New York 10, New York.

Preparation for "soul winning" may have been the language of a former day to describe leadership education for church school outreach. Training for educational or "fellowship" evangelism perhaps sounds a bit different, but the idea is essentially the same. A church that has lost its evangelistic passion becomes a mere club or society of human beings. Christian education without a deep and abiding desire at the center to share the " good news " with those who have it not tends to become mere formal and futile routine.

Chapter IX

AUDIO–VISUAL AIDS IN LEADERSHIP EDUCATION

Audio-visual education is as old as man himself. In primeval days instruction was by word of mouth, supplemented with certain crude signs and figures. For centuries good teachers of a more civilized society have made use of models, maps, charts, graphs, pictures, and blackboards to illustrate the spoken word and enliven the printed page. Modern recordings and projected visuals merely refine and extend the opportunities in this type of teaching-learning experience. We shall be concerned, in the pages that follow, with both the training of leaders *in* the use of audio-visual aids and the preparation of workers *by* means of this tool.

TRAINING LEADERS IN THE USE OF AUDIO-VISUALS

It is wise to begin with the appointment of an audio-visual committee. This group should derive its authority either from the governing body of the local church or from its general board of Christian education. The primary function of this committee would be to integrate the use of audio-visuals as a part of the regular and ongoing program of the church. Qualified educators, as well as persons with special interest in promoting the use of audio-visuals, should be members of such a committee.

A clear conception of the church's total task is of supreme importance. First meetings of the group might well be devoted to getting a comprehensive view of what the church is trying to do.

The pastor, or director of religious education, should be responsible for giving the instruction needed. On all matters the committee would be expected to clear through the body that appointed it.

Some of the essential tasks of the audio-visual committee are suggested by the Division of Christian Education, N. C. C. C., in its bulletin *Using Audio-visuals in the Church*,[1] whose excellent material is summarized at several points in this chapter.

1. *Investigate* the whole subject of audio-visual materials and methods by reading, consultation, and experimentation.

2. *Educate* members of the church in the meaning and value of audio-visuals.

3. *Study* the program of the church in its various aspects in cooperation with other workers to see where audio-visuals may best support the program.

4. *Develop* policies such as priority of equipment, use, rental clearance, and selection of pictures.

5. *Provide for a budget.* Permanent audio-visual equipment should be bought in the same way as other permanent equipment. Materials such as records, slides, filmstrips, and films may properly be added as an item to the budget for literature, supplies, or library. A long-range financial policy should include such expenditures in the church budget. As a temporary measure, special donations may need to be secured.

6. *Appoint a librarian,* who will keep a file of sources; consult with those who ought to use audio-visuals; order all films, filmstrips, slides, recordings, etc., and return them promptly; file and issue as needed all materials owned by the church. This person might also be the general librarian of the church school.

7. *Appoint a custodian for equipment,* who will keep all equipment in good working order and issue it to authorized persons as needed.

8. *Train voluntary operators* of all equipment and license them, when properly trained, to operate it.

9. *Provide a program of training and demonstration* for church leaders so that they will make proper and effective use of audio-visuals in teaching situations.

Careful reading of this list reveals that one of the committee's largest assignments is that of educating members of the church in the meaning and value of audio-visual aids and training leaders in their use. Consideration of the following questions will help in achieving this goal.

What types of audio-visuals are being used successfully by the churches?

[1] A manual for the local church audio-visual committee.

1. Projected materials:
   a. Still pictures: *opaque materials, transparent slides of various types, filmstrips* (usually 35 mm. and in either single or double frame) with captions and recordings.
   b. Motion pictures (usually 16 mm.): *sound* and *silent.*
2. Nonprojected materials: *charts, graphs, maps, posters, blackboards, bulletin boards, printed pictures, turnover charts, dioramas.*
3. Recordings and transcriptions: *disc recordings* (usually 78 or 33⅓ r.p.m.), *wire recordings, tape recordings.*
4. Radio, television, facsimile.

Stage presentations and other forms of nonprojected, nonrecorded dramatic productions are not to be regarded as audio-visuals, nor are pamphlets, booklets, and books.

What is the purpose of audio-visual aids in a program of Christian education?

These tools, when skillfully handled, serve to make instruction more interesting, more vivid, and more permanent. There is abundant evidence that when carefully chosen materials are properly used, the goals of the church are more effectively achieved. Audio-visuals, as an aid to teaching, promote faster learning, longer and more accurate retention. This experience is verified both by the observation of workers who have used them and by the scientific testing of results.

Always we should remember that audio-visuals are only one means of helping to convey the truth. Variety in the use of teaching techniques is a basic principle. There is no *one* method or *one* type of material that will achieve all the purposes of the church. Audio-visual aids are valuable when co-ordinated with other devices. But overemphasis upon them may reduce the effectiveness of carefully prepared curriculum materials provided by the Christian education agencies of the various denominations. The personality of the leader, the learner's own study and activity, the power of God's Holy Spirit, all are needed in effective teaching. A "nothing else but" attitude introduces the killing influence of monotony. Best results follow from a combination of approaches designed to fit the needs of the group under guidance and the nature of the lesson to be taught.

Are there fundamental principles to be observed in the use of audio-visuals?

Three have been suggested by expert workers in this field:

1. Adequate preparation of the student for what he is about to do, see, or hear.

2. Careful environmental adjustment so that the aid will be used under the most favorable circumstances.

3. Prompt follow-up of the experience — a discussion, a paper, an activity, or some sort of expression from the class. Satisfactory application can never be taken for granted. Individual participation in some form is essential to learning.

We turn again to the manual of the Division of Christian Education, N. C. C. C., *Using Audio-visuals in the Church,* for specific steps in the best use of audio-visuals.

Determination of Purpose: What is to be accomplished in the light of the total program of the church? How may this particular thing best be done? Is there an appropriate place for audio-visual aids?

Selection of Medium: What type of audio-visual can best help to achieve the specific purpose? Should a motion picture be used or a filmstrip or a record or some other type of material? Is it feasible to use it in the given project? Some situations do not lend themselves to using the medium best suited to the purpose, so that the next best may have to be used.

Selection of Specific Materials: What is available? Where can a reliable evaluation be secured? (The *Audio-visual Resource Guide for Use in Religious Education,* a publication of the Visual Education Fellowship of the Division of Christian Education, N. C. C. C., $1.50, is a reliable listing.)

Booking of Material: Reserve material and equipment for the desired date. Do it early — three to six months ahead.

Leader's Preparation: Preview material. Study how it may be most effectively used. Plan the session: time schedule, before and after discussion; tests of effectiveness to be applied; follow-up; are all important.

Room Preparation: Everything should be in readiness, with the group properly seated. For maximum smoothness of program, prepare the room early.

Group Preparation: Since these eye and ear tools are used to a purpose, care must be taken that they get the right setting with the group. Always this requires some statement of purpose. Sometimes it requires discussion before the showing, or presenting a number of questions to sharpen up observation. This preparation may be at the preceding session of the group, and, more often, just before the material is used.

Presentation of the audio-visual should be in connection with the unit of learning.

Follow-through: Make sure the purpose is achieved and the learning related properly to the pupil's experience. Educational use of audio-visuals is not the same as entertainment uses. The materials should be interesting, but the question, " How did you enjoy the picture? " (or record) is never in order.

Testing: Provision should be made for some sort of formal or informal test to discover change of attitudes and habits.

Does not all this make for more work than simple oral teaching? Of course! But it also makes for *less* work. It makes the presentation easier and more explicit, leads to more effective learning, and is always worth the effort.

What guideposts are to be followed in the purchase of equipment?

Most churches are still advised to buy first the necessary equipment for effective use of nonprojected visuals — such things as blackboards, models, maps, easels, pictures, and samples of religious art. In the case of projected visuals, the following items are suggested for purchase in the order listed:

1. Portable 70″ × 70″ beaded projection screen mounted on a tripod. This is desirable to provide for maximum use of both vertical as well as horizontal slides and filmstrips.

2. Combination 2″ × 2″ slide and filmstrip projector with a 5″ lens. (Where long throws, more than fifty feet, are necessary, a 7″ lens is desirable.)

3. Proper room darkening and ventilation facilities.

4. Record and transcription player (for various speeds).

5. 16 mm. sound motion picture projector.

6. Metal projection stands.

7. Microphone.

8. Mounted wall screens in the rooms where audio-visuals will be most frequently used.

9. Opaque projector.

10. Auxiliary lenses for slide and filmstrip and motion picture projectors.

11. Auxiliary lenses and speakers if needed for 16 mm. projector.

12. Magnetic recorder.

13. Filing and storage cabinets for audio-visual material.

What are the most usual mistakes in the use of audio-visuals?

Too much emphasis on the sound motion picture: This is the most expensive type of projected material which does not always lend itself to a valid educational experience. The filmstrip with record is probably the most effective teaching aid. The picture can be held longer on the screen and returned to as often as is necessary. Besides, the record usually provides a better spoken commentary than most teachers can give.

Bungling use of equipment often sidetracks interest and prohibits a genuine learning experience. Preliminary rehearsal will insure proper timing, correct order, and convenient location of materials, all of which are essential to an attractive presentation. Failure to have a spare lamp on hand, for example, may prevent the effective use of a projected piece of material.

Poor scheduling may defeat the purpose of a carefully chosen audio-visual. Good teaching procedure demands enough time for the discussion, action, or follow-up needed to integrate the presentation with the general program of Christian education. If a piece of audio-visual material requires a running time equal to or longer than the period for a given unit of study, some other type of material should be used.

Faulty ventilation frequently severely mars the effective use of a good audio-visual aid. A crowded group of sleepy people is far from a desirable learning situation. Hence, if the room must be darkened, be sure to provide some means for circulating the air. Automatic ventilation, of course, takes care of this problem.

Inadequate previewing: Successful use of audio-visual aids depends, in a very large degree, upon adequate preview. Failure to follow this rule may result in embarrassment, presentation of highly undesirable material, or loss of opportune learning. The leader must be familiar with all the content of material before it is used as a teaching tool.

Unsuitable selections result from scanty preliminary planning. The subject matter of audio-visuals should contribute toward achieving expected goals of Christian education. Use of technically excellent or colorful materials, merely because they are interesting and easily available, is a mistake. The leader must know how the particular medium he has chosen will serve the purpose of the church and promote the progress of the group for which it is designed.

Where can information and suggestions be secured by local church leaders?

The best source of help at the present time is the Department of Audio-visual and Radio Education of the Division of Christian Education, N. C. C. C., 206 South Michigan Avenue, Chicago 4, Illinois. Many of the ideas advanced in this chapter have been gleaned from its publications. A splendid service of the Department is the Visual Education Fellowship. The regular membership fee includes the *Audio-visual Resource Guide,* the *V.E.F. Newsletter,* and monthly *Evaluation Bulletins.* Selected listings, ratings, resource information, special programs; reliable suggestions concerning equipment, workshops, and institute plans, are provided for members of the Visual Education Fellowship.

The Religious Film Association, 45 Astor Place, New York 3, and Protestant Film Commission, 220 Fifth Avenue, New York 1, are in position to supply available information. Other sources of guidance are councils of churches and directors of audio-visual education on the national staffs of the various denominations.

PREPARATION OF WORKERS BY MEANS OF AUDIO-VISUAL AIDS

The previous section dealt with helping leaders to learn how to employ these aids for better results in their own specific activities. We now turn to the use of the techniques of audio-visual education as a general means of leadership education in the local church. Perhaps a practical demonstration is the best approach to this problem.

A group of denominations working through the Division of Christian Education, N. C. C. C., have recently produced a *Leadership Education Audio-visual Kit.* A statement of the nature and purpose of this series of audio-visual aids appears in the General Guide. They are designed:

1. To help prospective and experienced teachers to see the importance of teaching, realize the need for training, develop the skill needed, and receive inspiration.

2. To help pastors, administrators, and other leaders of the local church program to see the importance of teaching and to assist them in recruiting and training workers for the church.

3. To make the best educational use of rooms and equipment.

Following is a partial analysis of where and when the units may be most profitably employed.

In Training Classes: In the local church, in synod sessions, or at other times; in regular leadership education schools, laboratory experiences, the Leadership Education Audio-visuals can be major resources in leadership courses. Look over the problems of the class to see where the audio-visual can help the group. Does the class need new ideas? more information? aid in solving a specific teaching problem? motivation or inspiration to stimulate or sustain interest in the course? The answers to these questions will help to determine where the audio-visual will be most effective. If information is needed, there will be a most appropriate time to receive it. If an audio-visual is selected to stimulate discussion, do not schedule it to close or summarize a study, but at a point where discussion can follow. Always plan for enough time to do more than see and hear the audio-visual. This may mean using only a part of it in a session. For instance, it is recommended that you schedule three sessions on " The Teacher Teaches " so that methods of teaching may be studied and discussed. The Guides for the individual units make specific reference to courses and what may be achieved by the audio-visual unit prepared to supplement those courses.

In Workers' Conferences or Institutes for: church workers in general, vacation church school teachers, weekday church school teachers, pastors, superintendents. The workers' conference has a dual purpose. It should provide opportunity to gain information and get new ideas as well as for fellowship and inspiration. The use of appropriate audio-visuals will help to achieve both in less time. The Leadership Education Audio-visuals may well be used in conferences whenever their content will contribute to the purposes of the conference. Just as at other meetings, a worship setting will enrich a workers' conference when audio-visuals are used. Select the worship theme and materials and correlate all items of the program. Do not attempt to show too much. Prepare the group to see and hear and to be ready to question and evaluate. In many cases, the filmstrip and recording can be used to start a discussion that will enliven the conference and make the workers feel a part of the group. Use the Guide to get help in leading the discussion. Make some plans for improvement in the church school along the line presented in the filmstrip before closing the discussion. If such plans need to be made at different age levels, divide into department groups to continue the discussion and planning.

In Church Committees, Councils, and Boards of Christian Education: Since the enlistment, selection, and training of workers is a primary task of the local church committee or board of Christian education, these groups will want early to become familiar with all these audio-visuals. Using the audio-visuals as a basis for discussing and planning, they become acquainted with them as a medium that they can use for training teachers and other workers. One unit, for example, " Leads to Leadership," will help the board or committee to review and improve their own work. Since these are the people who will be using the audio-visuals with others, it is important that they learn to use them most effectively. The discussion in the committee or board should center around the question, " What is the best way of using the audio-visuals with the other workers in our church? "

The Guides will help them in answering this question.

Step by step procedure for the use of these Leadership Education Audio-visuals is suggested by the General Guide:

INVESTIGATE AND SELECT

1. Consider your group and discover its needs.
2. Consider the various units and select the one that most adequately meets the needs of *your* group.
3. Consider the best time for using the unit. Choose a time that allows for discussion and planning in addition to seeing and hearing. If more than one session is needed, get this into your advance planning.

GET YOURSELF READY

1. Preview the filmstrip and listen to the recording. Be sure you are familiar with both.
2. Study the guide to get in mind what this audio-visual will do for your group, how to use it with your group most effectively, what equipment and other materials you will need, how to prepare your group and follow through.
3. Plan definitely for use of the time available, so that it is divided between preparation of the group, seeing and hearing the audio-visual, and discussion and planning with the group.
4. If you can, meet with the group well in advance of the time you plan to use the audio-visual.

GETTING YOUR GROUP READY

1. Let the group help to list questions and problems for which they will seek answers or solutions. This anticipates discussion and planning after seeing and hearing the audio-visual, and prepares the way for it.
2. Arrange for advance assignments and preparation.

SHOW THE FILMSTRIP AND LISTEN TO THE RECORDING

See specific Guide for each filmstrip for suggestions on how to present it.

DISCUSS AND PLAN

The group need a chance to talk over what they have seen. The Guide with each unit provides discussion questions, suggests activities and sources of additional information. Persons who might be discouraged because the pictured situation may seem far in advance of their own practice or situation should leave the session with plans for some definite first steps toward improvement.

One advantage of a filmstrip is that you can hold a picture as long as desired and turn back to it for discussion as often as necessary. Since the script is given in the Guide prepared for the unit, and each frame is numbered, the leader can readily find those frames which help in the discussion of questions raised in the session.

Further specific advice is offered in the General Guide for equipment needed, how to show one of the filmstrips, and how to take care of the Kit. Each individual Guide applies in abundant detail the comprehensive process indicated above. Specific suggestions are offered to the leader for preparing himself, room and equipment, and students for the showing of the filmstrip chosen for a particular purpose. A helpful outline of how to go back and pick out the major issues, with comments and questions is presented.

If instructions for the use of these audio-visuals are carefully followed, it is almost impossible to fail in securing a genuine educational experience for the workers toward whom they are directed.

Audio-visual aids for training purposes are constantly being refined and extended in both scope and manipulation. Will they continue to be misused or neglected as is so frequently the case at the present time? Let us hope we are ready to take the pains required to make them the powerful instrument they ought to be in transmitting the truth of the Christian gospel. Much depends upon how we prepare our leaders in and by their use.

Chapter X

SELF–DEVELOPMENT THROUGH INDIVIDUAL READING AND STUDY

The Library

A workers' library is one of the most neglected tools of leadership education in the local church. On the other hand, it holds almost limitless possibilities, when rightly used, for improving the service of the educational staff. The familiar claim that church libraries are a waste of money has long since been exploded. One must confess that the old-fashioned church library, which consisted largely of parishioners' castoff volumes, was pretty hopeless. But there is a new day in the building and use of church libraries. Listen to this story from the West University Methodist Church, Houston, Texas.[1]

The library was established in 1945 with the sole purpose of serving the church and its members. In addition to providing books, it has developed many special services for the enrichment of the church's program. With its growth it has become more than a library. Indeed, it is the cultural center of the church.

Volunteer librarians co-operate with church school workers and other leaders. New church literature and materials are analyzed as soon as received to discover the resource requirements for coming programs. Workers immediately get in touch with the library to borrow books, pictures, and other aids. Slides and film-strips are ordered by the library to be available at the right time. Throughout the year the librarians prepare "availability" lists. These include materials and appropriate studies for program committees; individual aids for workers in the children's division;

[1] *Bookmarks*, p. 2. Church Library Service, the Methodist Publishing House.

resources for the co-operative living series; suggestive materials for teachers and many other groups.

Book reviews frequently appear in the weekly church paper. Displays are put up from time to time in various classrooms. A representative from the library attends each meeting held at the church. Some books or materials suitable for the particular group are always in view where the meeting convenes.

Maps and other teaching aids have been centralized and made immediately available for use. Pictures from publications are mounted on construction paper and placed in folders labeled by countries. Short stories, poems, and other useful resources are also mounted. Helps related to Christmas and other special seasons are similarly collected and made available. A " picture exchange " is being developed. The library has assembled religious pictures of high artistic rating which are placed in the different rooms and changed about at the beginning of each quarter. Art programs are given from time to time in every department.

The library supplies a wealth of professional material, which individual teachers may use for personal development or the enrichment of their class work. Excellent textbooks are also provided for local leadership training courses.

" But," you say, " this is a special case. The average church would not be able to put on such an ambitious program of library service." Perhaps; the illustration is used to refute the fallacious argument that time and money spent on a church library is necessarily wasted — not as a counsel of perfection to be followed by every church. However, even our smaller churches, with a modest investment of funds plus genuine devotion and the exercise of ordinary intelligence, could go much farther in the direction of what this Houston church has achieved than they now imagine. The Southern Baptist Convention has a large number of very small congregations, many of them in village or open country. Yet no Protestant denomination is more vigorous in promoting library service for every local church.

A library can make the program of the church more attractive and vital to all its members. We live in a period when people are constantly seeking for accurate information. Books and magazines on religion are usually scarce around a public library. It is the duty of the church to supply them and offer guidance in their use. The church's educational leaders — teachers, administrators, officers — need tools with which to work. Basic helps in Bible study, books to increase the knowledge and skill of teachers, sources of enrichment for the church school curriculum, suggestions for worship and wholesome recreation — these are some of the materials to which Christian education workers should have ready access. Religious stories and fiction for young people, as well as books on the development of the spiritual life, may help to counteract the materialism of present-day secular literature. Guidance for adults as they struggle to remain Christian in the midst of a pagan world is also a function of the church library. Literally thousands of churches, large and small, are extending and deepening the influence of Christian teaching through effective library service.

Steps in Securing a Library

Intelligent planning comes first. Under the leadership, or certainly with the enthusiastic approval, of the pastor, the whole idea should be discussed by the church's board of Christian education. Out of that meeting should come the appointment of a library committee, representative of the various interests in the church. Problems such as the following will demand attention as this committee canvasses the local situation:

What shall be the major purposes of the library? How is it to be financed? Where can we house it? On what basis will books and magazines be chosen? Where can we find help in making the initial selection? What can be done to promote the widest possible use of the library? Most important of all, this committee will be responsible for finding an acceptable librarian and initiating policies that will make his or her work fruitful. This person may or may not have had previous training in library administration. But the man or woman chosen should be a lover of books, willing to learn library techniques, with a capacity to sense other people's needs, and able to give time and thought to the operation of the library.

The Library Budget

The church library will not be successful without systematic financial support. Books are expensive and church budgets are notoriously tight. However, large amounts of money are not essential. Modest beginnings with steady growth will yield satisfactory returns under wise leadership. More depends upon the character and usefulness of the books on the shelves than upon the number. Even at present prices, fifty dollars will purchase a very good start in a workers' library.

Since all the organizations and groups in the church will ultimately profit from the use of the library, all should contribute to its support. This distributes the financial burden and creates a wide circle of interest. Gifts should be headed by an appropriation from the church itself, in order to give general recognition to the worth of the library. Many individuals will also be ready to help in the campaign for library funds. Books, furniture, and magazine subscriptions make splendid memorials. Most denominational publishing houses give substantial discounts on purchases made by church libraries, particularly for the first order.

It is the duty of the library committee to make sure that all monies devoted to this purpose are properly accounted for. This means the preparation and approval of a budget at the beginning of the year, and a report to the congregation on receipts and expenditures at the end.

Location and Furnishings

Fortunate indeed is the church that has a room especially designed for a library and used for no other purpose. However, lack of space for a separate room should not offer discouragement. A classroom, a convenient corner, or even a hallway may be adapted to this function. Two things are important. The library should be readily accessible to all the members of the congregation. Someone has said that it ought to be located at, or near, the "crossroads" of the church. The other essential is good lighting.

Minimum equipment, if the library is to be successfully used, would include the following:

1. Open shelves, adjustable, if possible. A stack of seven shelves, three feet long, will accommodate 150 to 200 books.

2. A magazine and literature rack.

3. A bulletin board for attractive display of book notices and library services.

4. A desk for the librarian, with drawers for card catalogue and supplies.

It is desirable, if space permits, to have a separate cabinet for supplies and records, as well as reading tables and chairs.

In the average church today much of this furniture could be built by craftsmen who are members of the congregation. But if the church has the money to purchase modern library equipment, the investment is a profitable one.

Guiding Principles in the Selection of Books and Materials

It has been rightly said that a church library is not a *collection* but a *selection* of books. There are certain basic texts and reference works that have a place in every library. But churches differ in program and needs. Perhaps the following suggestions may guide in the choice of what should go on the shelves and in the magazine racks.

1. Strive, first of all, to meet the needs of those who do the work of the church — teachers, administrators, counselors, musicians, leaders of special groups.

2. Select books that will appeal to persons of different ages and interests.

3. Include books that minister to spiritual growth and personal enrichment. Church school teachers, for example, must know more than merely how to teach.

4. Provide some books dealing with great social issues.

5. Make available information that will supplement the official program of the church. The rapidly developing field of audio-visual aids is a good illustration.

6. Co-operate, as far as possible, with the public library, if there is one in the community, in order to avoid unnecessary duplication in purchases and to secure maximum circulation of important books.

7. In building up the library, take counsel with the denominational board of Christian education. Usually one of the executives
on the staff is clothed with authority in this field and can offer
practical suggestions for churches of different sizes and resources.

Publicizing the Library

The success of the library depends in large measure upon how
well informed the congregation is regarding the services it is prepared to render. The Methodists have compiled an excellent list
of things to do in advertising what the library has to offer the life
of the church. It is subscribed below.[2]

" 1. The pastor must be well informed about your library. Remarks
by him from the pulpit, in meetings, and on his pastoral visits can be
more helpful to the library than many other methods. Your minister
will be especially interested in books on Christian beliefs and personal
devotions and in books for congregational reading related to his ser-
mon topics.

" 2. The other leaders of the church should know about your library — what it has and how it can help the church members. Their
recommendations will do much to let people know about the library
and lead them to use it.

" 3. Occasionally the librarian will be granted a few minutes at
various meetings to explain the values and rules of the library, tell
about new books, and suggest materials that will be helpful to the
persons who are present.

" 4. Announcements about the library and its books can be made
from time to time in the church bulletin and in other printed materials that the church gives or sends to its members.

" 5. The use of a bulletin board is essential for your library. If possible, it should have its own board — perhaps just outside the library
room. On this bulletin board continuous news of the library may be
posted. When this is not possible, the librarian should arrange for
display space on the church bulletin board. Perhaps the best displays
for the library are posters and the jackets of new books. In any case,
bulletin board displays should be large, so that they can be read
easily and quickly. People do not usually stand at a bulletin board and
read minute and lengthy notices. Instead, they give it a quick glance
while passing by. The display must therefore catch the eye and give
its message hurriedly.

[2] *Your Church Library*. Church Library Service, the Methodist Publishing House.

" 6. Special displays in your library can be used to attract attention. A small stand holding new books can be used, or perhaps new books can be laid on a display table. When special functions are being held in the church or when some phase of the church program is being emphasized, your librarian will want to display the books on this program. Christmas, Easter, the Lenten season, and other Church festivals are opportunities for displays that your librarian will not want to miss.

" 7. Your local newspaper often will be glad to print news articles about your library. A news item about the opening of the library will be especially interesting. Your paper will also be glad to receive news about any special programs or services your library has, special announcements about books that are added to the library, and about gifts to the library.

" It will be well for the librarian to consult the editor of the local paper to find out from him his ideas about news items on the library that he would want, and how he would like such articles turned in to him. Some member of the library committee may be able to handle newspaper articles and certain other publicity items for the librarian. This is certainly one feature of the library service for which the library committee has as much responsibility as the librarian.

" 8. When the library is well established, and if the librarian has time, she will plan to carry out special library services. These may include a story hour for the children, a book review club for adults, or perhaps a marionette show. Some classes and groups in the church are quite apt to work with the librarian in providing some of these special functions.

" Each situation varies and your librarian will want to be alert to develop and carry out plans for promoting the use of the library, keeping in mind that ' the library is made for men and not men for the library.'

" 9. Occasionally the library will have special functions of its own. A dramatic skit or some other type of program on the library and its work may be given at one of the services of the church or church school. The library may hold open house or a tea when it is first opened or each year on the anniversary of its opening.

" The library is an integral part of the work of the church and like the church itself seeks to build the Kingdom of God. Since it is dedicated to this purpose, your minister may conduct a special dedication service when it is opened."

The Library and Leadership Education

The function of the library in a local church program of leadership education is perfectly obvious. If the demands of the various groups are being met, workers in the church will have at hand both resources for background study and tools to help in solving current problems. There will be available many suggestions for improving the programs of various church organizations. The pastor, director of religious education, general superintendent, or departmental superintendents may use the facilities of the library to provide guided reading for the beginning teacher, or fresh stimulation for the worker who has gone stale on the job. The library is the natural workshop of people who are taking leadership training courses, either in the local church or in a community school.

To churches that say they do not know how to begin, most of our denominations offer a selected list of books as a start, a sort of package library costing $50 or less. Almost any church, however small, can raise that much money for so vital a need. Frequently a substantial discount, or a few books free, are offered to churches that meet certain requirements.

A few current sources of book lists are given below. Write to your own denominational headquarters for further information.

1. *A $50 Leadership Education Library*. Presbyterian Church, U. S. A.

2. *Books for a Workers' Library*. United Lutheran.

3. *Building a Church School Library*. Christian Board of Publication, 2700 Pine Boulevard, St. Louis, Missouri.

CORRESPONDENCE COURSES

Time was when correspondence courses were held in contempt by people who thought that accurate learning could take place only in the physical presence of the instructor. But that day is gone. The adult education movement includes the offering of home study courses in all the arts, sciences, trades, and professions under the auspices of recognized educational institutions across the entire country. Churches alive to the possibilities of this long-distance study are providing correspondence work in the general program of leadership education. This experience is frequently a more rigid test of the student's ability and willingness to labor than the conventional class. The correspondence pupil gets called on every day.

High standards are maintained by denominations offering these courses. Assignments and written work are prepared by experienced leaders in the field of Christian education. Students use standard textbooks. The pupil receives explicit instructions as to what he must do to complete the course. Written reports are demanded, as well as thorough study of the textbook and certain other carefully selected references, if they are available. Most of the student's papers deal with practical problems or crucial issues raised by the course assignments. Arrangement is made whereby the pupil may receive formal credit for work satisfactorily finished.

Here are some of the advantages claimed for the correspondence method:

1. Persons who find it impossible to attend regular training classes have opportunity to improve both knowledge and skills.

2. The plan is flexible, in that the student may begin study at any time and make progress at his own rate of speed.

3. Courses may be chosen on the basis of individual interest and need.

4. Each student has the benefit of direct, continuous personal attention from the instructor.

5. The person taking a correspondence course has the privilege of choosing the most convenient times in his schedule for study.

6. The plan provides a variety of experiences in connection with the courses, which enrich the life of the pupil — guided reading, research, observation and experimentation, and practical participation in church work.

7. One of the best features of correspondence work is the fact that the student is thrown on his own resources. He must take the initiative, keep on the job, and bring his efforts to a final conclusion. He is compelled to discover his own difficulties and develop effective study habits.

8. Correspondence courses may be used to supplement other forms of leadership education.

Many Protestant denominations provide opportunities in this field. One of the most successful programs is that of the Methodist Church. Its Department of Leadership Education now offers more than ninety courses dealing with various phases of religion and Christian service. Comments received from people who take this work are most enthusiastic.

One woman from a small church in Massachusetts writes: " The group was the first of its kind ever held in our church and perhaps provided the foundation for further training work. It put a value on the privilege of teaching that the group had not had before." This was in reference to a course on " How to Teach in the Church School."

Suggestions for study and conditions for completion of a correspondence course are carefully outlined in the Methodist manual *Correspondence Courses for Church Workers.*

Suggestions for Study

Suggestions for study have been prepared for each course available by correspondence. They include suggestions for doing effective work; aims and purposes of the course; list of approved text and reference materials; topics and problems for study and discussion; suggested activities (individual and group) such as assignments for reading, observation, investigation, and written work. These " Suggestions for Study " are sent to each individual who enrolls, and to the leader, in a study group or class in the local church or in a district or conference-wide program.

Conditions for Completion of a Correspondence Course

1. Each student must have passed his fifteenth birthday, except in the case of specialization courses in the children's field (which are for persons above seventeen years of age) and a few of the youth division courses for adult workers with youth.

2. Careful reading and study of the approved text materials is essential. Full use should be made of additional resources wherever possible.

3. A study of the topics and problems and the pursuit of the activities recommended in " Suggestions for Study " are required. (Each student should give special attention to such activities as are related to his own church work and will help him to derive the

largest values from his study. Sufficient time should be spent in the study to consider the major topics that deal with the problems of the students. Some students find it desirable to spend many hours in the study of a course. However, courses should be completed within a reasonable length of time for effective work, and because changes are frequently being made in the courses as a result of developments in educational theories and practices.)

4. Sending to the Department of Leadership Education the reports called for in " Suggestions for Study."

5. Sending of enrollment fees or freewill offering in the case of groups.

Regular credit cards are given for work satisfactorily completed, and correspondence students can go on to the achievement of a Certificate of Progress.

Leadership education has hardly scratched the surface in the matter of guided reading and study for volunteer workers. Here is an opportunity to meet individual needs and develop qualified leaders wholly within the confines of the local church. While the individual served will need to check personal findings from time to time against group experience, steady progress can be made by the wise use of the library and skillfully directed correspondence courses. The church should come awake to the possibilities that lie in getting workers to take advantage of these tools.

CHAPTER XI

HELPING PARENTS IN RELIGIOUS LEADERSHIP

The place of the parent as a teacher of religion has been often emphasized. But Protestant groups have done precious little to train parents for this important task. Much has been written on the subject and many eloquent speeches have been made without significant, widespread response from the local church. One denomination (Presbyterian Church, U. S. A.) is making strenuous efforts along this line, because its church school literature calls for parental co-operation. Reports from the field indicate that, while some progress has been made, the going has been slow. There are genuine difficulties in the way, which must be faced with sympathetic understanding.

Recent investigation reveals that most Christian parents are desirous of helping their children in their religious growth, but do not know where to begin. A few are totally indifferent to their responsibility for this task. And it is a cause for rejoicing that there are some who are doing a grand job of teaching religion in the home. We may assume that non-Christian parents are not qualified for this function, since they are unable to speak with personal conviction. Here are some of the comments that were made: [1]

1. " Conferences for parents are needed such as those we have for teachers."
2. " Only one parent-teacher meeting; response not too good — no follow-through."
3. " Attitude of parents toward parent-teacher meeting held was poor — parents were not given a set of instructions."
4. " No Sunday school classes in our church for people of our age.

[1] Taken from recent research by the Presbyterian Church, U. S. A.

We miss something. I have nothing as a parent to prepare me for what I am supposed to give my child."

5. " Too many interruptions — most of us don't have regular times set for this purpose."

6. " Good church school material in more condensed form."

7. " Our congregation is not holding the interest of parents."

8. " We need parents' meetings regularly for interested persons. Disinterested ones should be contacted personally."

9. " Family neighborhood meetings for parents are needed."

10. " No specific guidance is given to parents; consequently, there is no follow-through on their part."

11. " Nobody has told me what I am supposed to do."

12. " Fathers in rural areas don't have time to work with children."

13. " There are no teacher visits in the home and no parents' meetings in our church."

14. " Public school homework is very heavy. Little time is left for studying church school materials."

15. " There is no program for parents other than a talk by the pastor. We don't know anything about the study course."

These frank comments from parents sharpen up the issue and remind us that there is a real challenge ahead for those who would make the home an effective agency in transmitting the Christian heritage. Certain facts stand out as basic considerations in any approach to the problem. Among them, the following are suggestive:

Parents are busy people. Meetings or conferences designed for their participation must be carefully planned and properly timed. If we are to make lasting progress with parents, they themselves must be persuaded and trained to take the lead. Occasional exhortation to parents is no longer effective, if it ever was. The church that expects to get anywhere in a parent program must be ready to compete with the new techniques and materials offered parents by secular organizations today. This means a lot of hard work, persistent effort, and critical thinking over a long period of time. Instruction for parents should begin where they are, recognizing their theological illiteracy. It should be simple, direct, and specific. Finally, the actual needs of parents, as far as we are able to discover them, should be the mainspring and the measuring rod of all that we attempt to do.

How Shall We Proceed?

Churches vary; hence, no counsel of perfection is advanced which will fit every situation. But a good way to begin in a democratic country such as ours is by seeking the co-operation of parents and Christian education workers in tackling the problem. Secure the appointment of a committee composed of interested people from both these groups. Ask this committee to survey the local church situation, in order to determine needs and present practice. The following check might spearhead the investigation.

Regarding the Church School Program

1. Enrollment and number of teachers in the department.
2. Names of teachers who are or have been parents.
3. Workers, not parents, who are well qualified for the task they are handling.
4. Other persons in positions of leadership who are immature or lacking in adequate training.
5. What is the record of pupils whose parents are: not members of the church? members of some other church? nominal or inactive church members? faithful members of the church? workers in the educational program of the church?
6. Does the church have any systematic plan of evangelizing unchurched parents of children in the church school?
7. What program does the church have for enlisting the leadership of parents in family religion through: organization, special classes, parent previews of lesson materials? literature on family worship and teaching religion in the home? special occasions, such as premarital counseling, the birth of the baby, the dedication service or the baptism of infants, the first Communion, family night?

An excellent self-check list for getting this information about parental co-operation is suggested in *Home and Church Work Together*.[2] Parents are asked to check practices in accord with their own habits.

[2] P. 12. Division of Christian Education, N. C. C. C.

Having discovered the needs, this committee has the duty of recommending ways and means of training parents to assume their essential role in the spiritual nurture of their children. It should survey the best literature on parent education and Christian family life (source material listed at the end of this chapter), choose the approaches that can be best adapted for use in their church, and suggest specific action leading to the adoption of a co-ordinated plan. Only a few of the methods that have been successfully used across the country can be developed here, but many others will be found in the references mentioned above.

Parent-Teacher Meetings

Following is a portion of a letter that describes one way in which effective parent-teacher meetings have been planned and carried out:

" We have had such a good year with our new parent-teacher group that I felt you might like a brief outline of our program for reference in case any other church would be interested in trying one.

" A little over a year ago our junior superintendent, Mrs. Ernest Humphries, who for some time had felt there was a need for a parent-teacher group, arranged an afternoon meeting for the mothers and teachers in her department. She had an excellent program: a hobby show which the juniors had arranged and which the mothers judged; two talks on the essentials of building Christian character and some of the problems in child growth; and a social period with tea and cake. At that meeting she asked if the group would be willing to be organized. A nominating committee was appointed, and at the May meeting — which was an evening meeting, to include fathers — four officers were presented and elected: president, vice-president, secretary, and treasurer. These officers proceeded from that point.

" The vice-president, a father but not a teacher, became chairman of the program committee. This committee was composed of two women — one a teacher, one not — and three men, two of whom were teachers. We have tried very hard not to burden the church school teachers. Through the year this committee met along with the officers and was called our planning committee. The minister also sat in when possible. This planning committee was the keystone of our organization. It was an excellent group, and perfectly marvelous ideas came forth whenever it got together. We decided to name our group — following the idea of the curriculum materials — Church and Home Council. At first it began as a junior parent group, then became a general church school group. Now we include all parents and teachers of our more than 400 church school children from kindergarten through senior high. Our largest attendance is from the primary and junior departments.

" Our programs have been varied, but have kept continually in mind that we are a parent-teacher group working for the better Christian education of our children. We have continued to meet in the evening, once a month, because that means that the men and the teachers who work during the day can attend. We have very brief business, following an opening hymn and prayer, and go directly into the program. After the program, which we try to keep within an hour, we have cake and coffee served by a committee. Our treasury consists solely of the coins dropped into a dish to defray the expense of the cake and coffee. We have been subsidized by the church to the extent that if we need to pay for a film or a speaker, that will be taken care of. We have not needed that as yet because our best programs have come from our own group.

" These are some of our programs:

" A panel on ' Your Child and Prayer ' led by four parents, with discussion from the floor.

" A group conference evening. We had 5 discussion groups led by 5 leaders, all laymen, on the general topic ' Your Child — a Growing Christian? ' Each group took a smaller part of that question for discussion, i.e., ' Is your child growing in his relationship to God? to the Bible? to his community? ' etc. The groups were out for about 25 minutes, then returned and one person reported from each. It was an excellent meeting — everyone had a chance to say something. We met with the group leaders a few days before the meeting to discuss methods of leading discussion groups.

" A formal debate — 6 debaters discussed the question suggested in *Counsel* one month, ' Resolved, that religious education should be made available in the public school.' Over 70 people turned out for that one — we had a timer, 3 judges, and proceeded in the best scholastic manner. The debaters had put a lot of time on it — so far we feel it to be the best meeting of the year.

" Our pastor spoke one evening on ' How Does a Boy or Girl Acquire a Real Christian Faith? ' — gave parents something new to think about.

" The Methodist minister gave a talk on the literature of the Bible.

" A crowd of 150 packed in one evening recently when the junior department put on a program, each class presenting briefly the work they had accomplished during this year from their curriculum material

" We expect to close the season next month with a Bible quiz in which everyone will participate.

" We have tried to stick to general problems that all families encounter in trying to raise children these days, problems relating to their character education.

" Our biggest difficulty is getting effective publicity to the parents. We finally devised a system of class mothers, in which there is one chosen from each class; before each meeting that mother receives a card with the announcement about the coming meeting and she is asked to invite the other parents of her child's class. That has worked fairly well. We feel that we should recommend for another year that there be a publicity chairman, with possibly a committee to help to keep the lists up to date and to work out new ways of contacting parents. We feel that the fellowship of parents and teachers is one of the most important phases of the group."

Certain things stand out quite clearly in this report. The first is that the church was not willing to give up easily. Furthermore, parents took an active part in the planning and programs. The minister gave his official support from the beginning. The meetings were varied in character, but all contributed to the general purpose of giving practical help to parents faced with problems in the Christian education of their children during these times. The whole venture was closely correlated with the work of the church school. Publicity proved to be the biggest headache. However, the ingenious system of class mothers largely overcame the difficulty.

Home Visitation

One of the most effective ways of securing parent co-operation is through visitation in the home. This procedure can be and often has been a waste of time. But there is no reason why it should not be as carefully planned and fruitfully consummated as any other phase of the church's work.

Who should do the calling? Church school teachers are a natural, because of the contact and understanding that should exist between the church and the home. Parents may also be trained to help with the visiting. Often they can relieve overburdened teachers, and, besides, the parent-to-parent contact may get a response that is beyond the reach of the teacher.

What should take place when a call is made? Obviously any attempt to dictate behavior in a personal relationship of this kind would be foolish. However, evangelistic calling has profited from the guidance of experience, and it seems sensible to utilize the suggestions of those who have been successful at it.

1. A call that is evidently perfunctory or chiefly social will not get us very far. Most parents welcome the opportunity to talk about the spiritual welfare of their children.

2. Information about the background of the child, which will be helpful in his religious instruction, should be sought.

3. The visitor ought to be ready to explain the purpose and the program of the church school.

4. Parents should be made familiar with lesson materials and told quite explicitly how they can co-operate in teaching the truth they are intended to convey.

5. The visitor should have on hand a list of references dealing with the problems most frequently raised by parents — how to hold family worship, for example.

When shall we go calling? " Any old time is a good time to talk religion " may or may not be true. Certainly, better results will be obtained with parents if the home is not indiscriminately invaded. More will be accomplished if the visit can be arranged ahead of time, so that both father and mother can be present. That implies an evening call, as a rule. Some churches set two or three seasons in the year when home visitation becomes a major project. If parents know that the call will be worth-while, they are usually co-operative in providing a convenient time.

What follow-up is desirable? If the visit is to produce any lasting results, a record should be made of it, with action taken on the information gathered. Some churches use mimeographed report sheets for this purpose. When parents do the calling, they ought to report their findings to the teachers concerned with the children in the home. Information on materials requested by parents should be carefully noted and supplied promptly afterward.

Planning with Parents for Teaching

Some churches are challenging their parents by offering a superior program of Christian education for their children, with handles where they can take hold. This frequently takes the form of parent-staff conferences, at which church school materials are studied and the part parents should play in the teaching carefully pointed out. Parents also register other difficulties and suggest possible improvements in the literature and teaching aids, when viewed from their standpoint. Suggestions for conducting such a preview are found in *My Lesson Planning Book.*[3] The substance of that section appears below.

Sample of Procedure in Conducting a Parent Preview

Experience has shown that it is wise to hold departmental parent previews in some couple's home rather than at the church, if feasible, and that even when there are general parent meetings at the church, the group should be divided departmentally for most of the time, to do the following:

1. Have a short devotional period, followed by appropriate introductions.

2. See that everyone has appropriate materials for the quarter in hand.

3. Describe in some detail the actual content and subjects to be covered during the quarter.

4. Highlight the aims of the quarter's work, pointing out where they are stated or implied in the materials. Wherever possible, underscore the most important truths, knowledge, attitudes, and skills sought as outcomes. Show how what the boys and girls learn ties in with the big things required of a disciple of Christ.

5. Turning to the long-range quarterly chart worked out preceding the preview meeting, indicate to the parents what will be " doing " on specific Sundays. Give them a vision of the work. Wherever alternate procedures are indicated in the materials, have parents mark the one that has been chosen for use.

6. Home assignments: Make clear to the parents exactly what is

---

[3] Pp. 8, 9. Board of Christian Education, Presbyterian Church, U. S. A.

expected of them in this respect. Explain clearly parents' participation in memory work, special projects for an individual student
or a class, parents' relationship to activity materials, how they can
stimulate their children to prepare for the coming Sunday, and
in what ways the teachers are able to help them do their part.

7. Evaluation period: Stimulate thinking with questions like
these: Do you feel that the lessons are getting across to your
child? Is he learning? Is he growing as a Christian? Are there
things we could do together to strengthen the department? At
what points do you feel the need of more help? How can we get
more parents to participate? What are you yourself willing to do
to achieve this objective? Would it be wise to set aside certain
Sundays for parent visitation in the classrooms?

8. Have ready a list of inexpensive aids and books that may be
used to promote personal spiritual growth. For example: *Today*,
a monthly magazine for personal devotions (The Westminster
Press); *Five Minutes a Day*, compiled by Robert E. Speer (The
Westminster Press); *Opening the Door for God*, by Herman J.
Sweet (The Westminster Press); *Our Family Grows Toward
God*, by Mary C. Odell (Abingdon-Cokesbury Press); *The Faith
of Our Children*, by Mary Alice Jones (Abingdon-Cokesbury
Press); also the leaflet *Ways of Worshiping in Our Homes*, by
Kardatzke and Phillips (Department of Adult Work, Presbyte-
rian Board of Christian Education). All may be ordered through
denominational bookstores.

9. Whenever possible, use visual aids, charts, pictures, maps.
Do some of the things that will be expected of the pupils. Make
the parents feel that they are participating in a genuine experience. *Never make this preview so long that the parents become
exhausted.* Most of them will have been at work all day. Light
refreshments might be served at an appropriate time.

The Myers Park Baptist Church, Charlotte, North Carolina,
which has been a leader in this movement, makes the following
appeal to parents on the report of pupil progress, which it sends
out periodically:

" It has been a distinct pleasure to have your child in the educational program of our church. We hope sincerely, whether the grades
shown here be high or low, that he will have developed greatly in

Christian personality, for it is such progress that we hold as the goal of our program.

" The tests have been so designed as to instigate student thinking of the caliber that will promote this end. The study question plan was begun in order that there might be frequent occasion and opportunity for this thinking to take place in the home and within the family circle, and in order to achieve family conference and discussion on the subjects of needed consideration for Christian personality development. The tests, given on Sunday morning, are a means of measuring how well the students have learned to think out such specific phases of their own philosophy of life. The test grades, then, are indications, not of possession of, or lack of possession of, factual material, but rather, something of an idea of the degree of progress your child has made in meeting, and in evaluating the best reaction to, given situations.

" You may be of much assistance in this program. Will you not make it possible for your child to be present regularly at every function designed for his group? Will you not encourage careful consideration of the church school lesson material and of the study questions in the family circle, and, through your interest and attention, help him better to prepare for the other activities in which he participates? Will you not avail yourself of the opportunity of our parent-staff conference to learn better to understand our church program and to understand how you may best use it and co-operate with it for the greatest benefit of your child? And will you not feel that your church staff is personally interested in you and your family and that it seeks opportunities to know and meet your needs and to understand and solve your problems? Together we will prepare your child with such a wholesome, well-rounded, Christian attitude toward life that whether he goes to college, into business, or directly into a home of his own, he will be well grounded in his thinking and able to meet any situation, to evaluate it without prejudice, to take from it the good for his own, and to present to others through all of his living, the attractiveness of the Christian way of life."

Another church has stimulated interest in parent-staff conferences by the use of what it calls a " *Parents' Covenant Form.*"

FIRST PRESBYTERIAN CHURCH SCHOOL, CASPER, WYOMING

Parents' Names _____	Church Member ____ Where ____
Address _____	Telephone _____
Child's Name _____	Birth Date _____
Grade _____	Church Member _____

For the Religious Nurture of Your Child:

The Church Agrees to the Following Six Points:
1. To furnish a room at the church and adequately equip it for the use of your child.
2. To make this room available to your child each Sunday morning between 9:45 and 10:45.
3. To provide competent Christian men and women who will lead your child in his thinking and worship during this hour each Sunday.
4. To regularly provide religious books and pictures and other teaching materials for your child.
5. To do everything possible to teach your child to love the Christ, his church, and his home, and all other people.
6. To conduct a parent-teacher conference once every three months so that parents and teachers may better co-operate for the training of your child.

Church School Superintendent _____
Church School Department Superintendent _____
Pastor _____

We Parents Agree:
( ) 1. To have our child at the church school each Sunday morning at 9:45 o'clock, *unless providentially hindered.*
( ) 2. To secure, and diligently use, the teacher-parent magazine, a study of which will help us and our child's teacher to work together for his religious development.
( ) 3. To teach our child to pray by praying with him privately, before meals, and in family worship.
( ) 4. To teach our child the proper stewardship of money and to train him to bring his weekly contribution.
( ) 5. To keep our child's church school reading book in a safe place and guide him in the wise use of it.
( ) 6. To attend the parent-teacher conference which will be held at the church once every three months, *unless providentially hindered.*
( ) 7. To assume our family's share in financing the educational program of our church according to the plan adopted.

Parent's Signature _____

_____
(Both parents, if possible)

Experience has shown that participation of parents in a program of this kind is increased if the meetings become neighborhood affairs. Gathering in the home of a friend is not only more convenient, but firsthand acquaintance makes discussion easy. Under such circumstances, a committee of parents is responsible for administrative details, publicity, and refreshments. One caution — it is easy for a meeting of this sort to become a mere social bull session.

Special classes for parents, premarital counseling, the dedication service or infant baptism, and pastoral guidance in family relationships are other means of successful parent education. One gets the impression that not many churches are working very hard at this job. But where a church takes its obligation to help parents seriously, the response of this group is as good as any other. Persistence, patience, and planning, in which parents have a hand, will bring surprising results.

More detailed information on helping parents in religious leadership may be found in the following publications:

Home and Church Work Together. Division of Christian Education, N. C. C. C.

Parent Education and Christian Family Life (excellent bibliographies in connection with several chapters). The Westminster Press.

Teaching Religion in the Home, by G. W. and R. M. Brown. The Westminster Press.

Chapter XII

SUPERVISION — COACHING

What Do We Mean by Supervision?

The word "supervision" conveys a distasteful meaning to the minds of many teachers and workers. Certain types of tyrannical overlordship in business, and the bungling of public-school administrators here and there, have contrived to give the idea a bad name. Teachers often use such expressions as the following when discussing the term: "checkup," "spying around," "dictation," "picking flaws," "supervision, bah, you mean snoopervision." We begin on this negative note in order to dismiss from our minds immediately any such concept of supervision.

Fortunately, the church cannot practice for long any kind of supervision that smacks of the inquisitorial or autocratic. Most of its workers are volunteer helpers. They are to be led and encouraged, not driven. Simply stated, supervision for our purposes is the measurement of teacher effectiveness with suggestions for improvement. It thinks of this process as a mutual enterprise, in which the opinions of the worker are as highly respected as those of the guide. Its purpose is not to give orders, but to encourage growth and the achievement of independence. Supervision aims at improving the quality of the service rendered to the church. Its ultimate goal is intelligent, democratic leadership that promotes spiritual development of both teacher and pupil. We do not mean to imply from this that the function of supervision is discharged by an occasional pat on the back. Teachers do appreciate the spoken word of thanks. But they welcome even more heartily practical, down-to-earth assistance on the problems that they face as Christian leaders. Supervision that pays dividends must be realistic as well as sympathetic. It expects the person being supervised to receive with good cheer constructive, friendly criticism and to act upon it. At the same time, the co-operative nature of supervision, as we have described it, produces creative insights, which do not appear in an " I-give, you-take " relationship.

WHO WILL BE THE SUPERVISOR?

First-class supervisors who can do what we have suggested are rare anywhere. The church has not trained many technical experts in this field. However, helpful guidance is still possible in most churches, if people are willing to learn and work together in the spirit of Christian patience. Frequently, the minister will be the only person qualified to undertake the work of a supervisor. Departments of religious education in some seminaries are preparing young ministers very adequately for this task. However, preachers who have little interest in the church school, or those who are temperamentally unfitted for the job, will do more harm than good. If the church has a director of religious education, that person is expected to be qualified for supervisory duties. Sometimes the general superintendent has gifts and training along this line. He has to be careful that he does not equate administrative functions with instructional supervision. Departmental superintendents are always clothed with supervisory responsibilities. There is urgent need that most of them take summer school courses, which will fit them better to serve in this capacity. In a large number of churches there are public-school people who have had special education and experience as supervisors. If they are equally devoted as Christians, their leadership is always valuable.

SETTING UP STANDARDS

The first step in supervision is to find a measuring rod with which to calculate success or failure in a given educational program. All workers are judged, whether or not they wish to be. The questions that supervision raises are: By what standards are they rated? How fair is the judgment of their performance as interpreted in the light of the standards? There are many instruments for testing the effectiveness of church school work, ranging all the way from a general statement of desired results to a detailed outline of specific items that go to make up a particular function. A sample is given below.[1] There are certain general tests which every conscientious leader applies to his work. Many of these have some real value if used with discrimination.

Earmarks of Successful Work

1. One of the first that occurs to us is the pupil's interest in his work, and in religious subjects generally. If he listens attentively, asks intelligent questions, and answers questions with a mark of understanding, we assume that his religious life is growing happily and that our work with him has been well done.

2. One of the conspicuous ways in which interest manifests itself is in good attendance and in punctuality.

3. As another mark of success, lesson preparation will come in for large consideration.

4. Almost without exception, Sunday school teachers would rate high as a mark of successful teaching the knowledge that the pupil has acquired. We must, of course, remember that there are more important tests than mere Bible knowledge. The ultimate test is character and conduct. Yet it is a good policy to assume that unless teaching leads to a definite broadening of the horizons of knowledge, it is not likely to yield much extension of the scope and quality of attitudes and habits.

5. Since the final test of the success of a religious education is life, there are good reasons for looking to the daily conduct of pupils for evidence of successful teaching. The observation of pupils in home, school, and community, under proper conditions, is one of the best tests of results achieved.

6. Definite confession of Christ, and alignment with the church, is to most teachers the supreme test. It is difficult for any individual teacher to apply this, because confession of Christ and joining the church are the culmination of the work of many teachers. All teachers may take credit for the pupils who gloriously pass this test and all should share the blame with others for those pupils who fail.

These are some of the common-sense tests that we apply to measure the success of Christian teaching. The very fact that a teacher has a sufficiently critical attitude toward his work to wish to estimate its success is in itself a wholesome sign. He must

---

[1] *Improving Your Sunday School,* by Paul H. Vieth, pp. 151–153. The Westminster Press.

make his judgment on the basis of the best evidence he has. Excellent rating scales both for the individual leader and for the general work of the church are found in *And Gladly Serve*, a publication of the Division of Christian Education, N. C. C. C.

The Christian education staff in the local church will find its spirit and outlook substantially changed, if it will address itself over a period of time to the construction of its own tools of measurement. Out of such an experience can come a whole new concept of the importance and purpose of Christian nurture, as well as clear understanding of what supervision would like to achieve. This develops into a continuous process of self-improvement as the group sets up standards of achievement in various phases of church work — worship and recreation, for example — and revises them from time to time as changing situations may demand.

SOME TECHNIQUES OF SUPERVISION

It will not be possible in this brief compass to discuss all the ways of giving helpful supervision to church leaders. But some of the most practical methods for use in Christian education will be briefly treated.

Coaching Teachers and Other Workers

By coaching in this connection we mean at least three things:
1. Helping those responsible for a certain task to plan intelligently.
2. Checking by observation on the steps or stages in the execution of the plan.
3. Adequate follow-up through evaluation of what happened.

Improving Worship Services

The first step is to begin where people are with a survey of present practice listing assets and deficiencies. This is a beautiful example of co-operative supervision, because the information needed can be supplied by a committee of those who have responsibility for worship programs. The supervisor's chief job here is to be sure that all the facts are revealed as to the content, the planning, and the holding of worship services.

Then the group should agree upon criteria by means of which to judge the effectiveness of programs designed for a valid worship experience. Many denominations have developed standards for this purpose. The following sample, worked out by the Division of Christian Education, N. C. C. C., may stimulate thinking.[2] It would have to be adapted perhaps to meet the needs of differing local situations.

" Worship should hold a central place in the program of the church school. Much care and attention must be given to the element of worship in the program so that it may lead pupils into a genuine experience of communion with God.

" 1. Are the periods devoted to worship kept free from such distractions as announcements, training in singing, unrelated addresses, whispering, talking, and other disturbances?

" 2. Are plans for worship carefully prepared in advance, taking into consideration the interests, needs, and ages of the pupils?

" 3. Do the programs usually have a central thought, with which the Scripture readings, hymns, music, prayers, and other elements are in harmony?

" 4. Do pupils have opportunity to assist in preparing and conducting the program? "

Once a standard has been accepted, the next step is to plan one or more worship experiences following carefully the suggestions contained in the guide. Plans on paper may look beautiful. But the only way to know whether they will work is to test them out with the group. When the worship service, so thoughtfully constructed in keeping with the standards set up, is actually used, the supervisor should be on hand to see how it goes. He will make note of successes and failures in the execution of the plan, jotting down alternative procedures that might have made the experience more genuine.

As soon after the program has been rendered as is convenient, the worker or the committee and the supervisor will sit down for an evaluation of the worship service. If others were observing the process, they should be in on this roundup too. Free give-and-take in the spirit of Christian understanding should characterize this

[2] *International Standard for the Sunday Church School.* Division of Christian Education, N. C. C. C.

conference. Often a teacher or worker with real insight knows more about why things went well or awry than the supervisor. Again the standard is used to provide a measure of objectivity in the exchange of ideas.

The Improvement of Lesson Preparation

This problem is handled in Chapter V. The procedure to be followed is essentially the same as that suggested above for the improvement of worship. The only thing to be added is the observation by the supervisor of the teaching process where the plan is used. It might be profitable to review Chapter V at this point.

Visiting with Workers on the Job: What we have been saying implies visitation of classroom and other activities. It is obvious that most churches will not find it possible to carry out the elaborate recommendations of the public schools for visiting the leader at work. On the other hand, casual " pop-ins " without purpose, plan, or follow-up will prove altogether futile. Teachers, as a rule, do not mind being observed if they know that helpful suggestions are likely to follow. But they see little point in just being watched. There are certain guiding principles that must be observed if maximum benefits are to follow from this joint endeavor for improvement. "Just common sense," you may say, when they are listed. But we have been a long time arriving at the use of common sense in human relations.

Pre-Teaching Conference: A good supervisor will not visit a class for observation without some prior knowledge of what the teacher plans to do and how he hopes to achieve his purpose. In the case of experienced workers, a brief oral interview may furnish all the information needed. But with beginners, or people having real difficulty, it is the function of the supervisor to help the person to think through both the content and the method he will use in the period under consideration. Together they may attempt to forestall certain difficulties or agree upon certain activities. *The plan should always be made by the worker.* However, it should be reviewed in conference with the aim of suggesting any revisions that may bring it more nearly in line with the needs of the group and good teaching procedure. This will be recognized as the third step in the coaching technique previously described.

How to Observe an Activity:

1. Come in quietly before the beginning of the period and find a place at the back of the room. Take no active part in the class-work. Some other occasion can be arranged for fraternizing with the pupils.

2. Stay for the entire time that the activity is in progress. No useful purpose is served by fragmentary observation.

3. Come prepared to take notes on everything that happens. A running narrative of events is very valuable for two reasons: (*a*) teachers or guides often do things unconsciously that they do not remember afterward; (*b*) this method of observation gives a measure of relief to the teacher, because he realizes that the supervisor is trying to be objective and is not merely jotting down unfavorable impressions.

4. Observation schedules have been prepared for all kinds of teaching-learning situations. Dr. F. M. McKibben's book [3] has a fine sampling. These are useful in calling attention to things to look out for during the period of visitation and as a help in analyzing the experience subsequently. But it is not always easy to follow an instrument of this kind during the progress of the activity.

Follow-up — the Interpretation and Post-Teaching Conference:
Having recorded the facts, the supervisor should make an analysis of what occurred as soon after the visitation is completed as possible. Here he will employ the standard previously agreed upon in arriving at judgments both favorable and unfavorable. He is under obligation at an early date to sit down with the person observed for a mutual review of the entire experience. When this takes place, greater progress will be made if the following suggestions are remembered:

1. Begin by inviting the teacher or worker to give his own impression of "how the day went." Encourage him to estimate his work, pro and con. Questions like the following can be used to keep the conversation on the track: "How do you think the plan worked out? Were you satisfied with the response of the pupils? At what points in the process did you have a distinct feeling of success? Were there any spots where you were disappointed with

[3] *Improving Religious Education Through Supervision.* Abingdon-Cokesbury Press.

results achieved? What would you do differently if you had to go through the experience again? If the supervisor succeeds in getting the person to talk freely, many things that he had planned to offer by way of remedial action will be gladly accepted by the worker during his own self-appraisal because the need is clearly understood. Care must be taken, however, not to put the person under supervision on the defensive.

2. When the supervisor's turn comes, it is good psychology to open up with commendation of all the things that the person observed did well. He can then pass more easily and objectively to discussion of the weak spots in the presentation.

3. Outlining corrective measures should be a joint project of supervisor and worker as they strive together for the very best performance of which the latter is capable. This may call for any number of adjustments. Perhaps some change in physical environment is needed. Often the worker will be asked to read pertinent literature bearing on a special problem. A weakness in classroom management may call for radical changes in teaching techniques. Or the teacher may need help in finding and using reference materials. Whatever the deficiency, the supervisor will not rest until the pathway of improvement is clear.

4. In all his dealings with the growing worker, the supervisor should use simple language; be sympathetic, patient, specific, factual, and willing to listen. The spirit of this process is even more important than any superior knowledge he may possess.

DEMONSTRATION TEACHING

Great benefit may be derived from watching a successful person conduct an activity, provided adequate briefing beforehand is given to those who observe, followed by thorough evaluation of the work after it is finished. This is the method of the so-called laboratory school, which is receiving so much emphasis as a training technique among all the Protestant denominations today. The student teachers help with the planning before the lesson starts. They observe experts as they guide the teaching-learning experience, and they join in the critique that follows.

Most local churches are not in a position to provide continuous laboratory instruction. But some form of demonstration teaching is available to all except the worst isolated. If there is a highly skilled teacher in the church school, his or her work may be observed from time to time by other leaders on the staff. Precaution must be taken not to interfere too frequently with the ongoing program of this person. The small church, without any trained leadership, may send a teacher occasionally to visit the classroom of an excellent instructor not too far away. There are both advantages and pitfalls in this form of leadership education. Little is to be gained in any case without careful supervision of the whole experience. Science makes constant use of the technique, but only under carefully controlled conditions.

Demonstration does put theory into practice. It shows how to apply the elements of a standard to a life situation. It tends to increase the confidence of those who observe. " I thought I couldn't do it, but Miss Black showed how easy it is." Good illustrations of how a thing should be done are always helpful and stimulating. One big advantage is the teachability (readiness to learn) of the observers. They come expecting to get many pointers that will ease them over some of the rough spots in their own teaching. This makes for alertness and insight.

The limitations of this procedure are readily apparent. One is the difficulty of securing a natural setting for the demonstration. Perhaps the problem is minimized in such activities as dramatics and recreation, where people are accustomed to being watched. But observation of a worship service can be very disturbing. Small children are likely to be less affected by visitors than are young people and adults. Of course, the larger the group of observers, the more artificial the teaching situation is likely to become.

There is danger that workers visiting in another church may go with an uncritical attitude, which blinds them to possible failures of the teacher visited. Here arises another handicap in this particular method of training. The supervisor may not find it easy to arrange the contacts needed to prepare for the visit and to evaluate the demonstration after the teacher returns. Furthermore, good substitute teachers are usually scarce. Every effort should be made, as soon as possible, to assure an observer of demonstration work the opportunity to put into practice what he has learned. There is no automatic transfer of skills from the expert to the novice through the mere process of watching. We learn to guide others by actually trying ourselves out with the new ideas we have acquired. The worker in service may go right ahead on this track without delay, but a place must be made for the cadet or apprentice.

In spite of the hurdles, observation of superior performance is generally approved by Christian educators as a fruitful means of developing better leaders in the Church. Its potentialities as a scheme of leadership training are greatly enhanced if it takes place under intelligent guidance.

THE LABORATORY SCHOOL

What has come to be known as the Laboratory School is an extension of demonstration teaching, with more refined techniques and often under more expert guidance. A good illustration of recent developments in this field for local churches is the program of the Presbyterian Church in the United States, known as the " Teacher Consultant Training Center Plan."

This recently inaugurated program of leadership education in the Southern Presbyterian Church came out of restudy and evaluation of the total offerings in Christian education across the denomination. It is described as a new approach in laboratory work, centering in the local church and conducted by local leaders. The basic philosophy is that those who train teachers should themselves be in close contact with real teaching situations comparable to those in which the learners are engaged. Teachers are helped most effectively through direct assistance in their classrooms or in closely similar situations. This takes place in two ways.

1. " Through opportunity to observe and at times to assist the teacher consultant at work in his (or her) training center.

2. " Through direct assistance of a teacher consultant who comes to help teachers where they are." [4]

[4] Leaflet entitled *On the Job Training*. Department of Leadership Education, Presbyterian Church, U. S.

Criteria for determining where these training centers shall be and who are to be designated as teacher consultants have been carefully worked out.

Criteria for the Training Center

" Approved Sunday school classes or departments in which: effective teaching is going on . . . Christian growth is taking place . . . there is genuine willingness to share with others for the good of all.

" Such centers will provide (for definitely specified length of time): apprentice training for beginning teachers . . . opportunities for observation . . . possible tie-up with Leadership Education courses.

" Observers will come by prearrangement as to numbers and dates; guide sheets will be supplied; conferences for evaluation should be arranged, if possible."

Criteria for the Teacher Consultant

" A new type of accredited teacher, who qualifies in one or more of the following patterns:

" I. Key person in charge of training center . . . who has demonstrated ability to teach effectively . . . who welcomes observers from the same or other churches . . . who can help other persons (apprentices) to learn how to teach . . . who can develop capable assistants, at least one of whom can take full responsibility during absence of teacher consultant.

" II. Key person in charge of a training center who can also go to neighboring churches on Sundays, as invited . . . to observe . . . to counsel with teachers . . . sometimes to demonstrate what could be done in that situation.

" III. Key person in charge of a teaching situation that fulfills to an acceptable degree the criteria established for a training center, although such a situation may not be open for observers. (This would probably occur most often in youth work.) It should, however, offer one important feature of the training center, namely, opportunity for an apprentice to assist the teacher consultant for a given period.

" IV. A person who has demonstrated ability to do effectively a certain kind of work in a practical, down-to-earth fashion. Although such person may not be actively in charge of a local group, he should maintain close and continuing contact with actual teaching situations. This category will probably include members of the educational staff (office and field), their assistants, other leaders in church school work." [4]

Following is a suggested plan for development of a training center in a local church:

"Work toward meeting the criteria as fully as possible, giving special attention to the development of capable assistants for the teacher consultant. Request evaluation and official recognition (from Department of Leadership Education, through your regional director) when group is ready and session of your church has approved the project. Open training center to observers, from your own and nearby churches. Parents as well as teachers might be invited. Consult with regional director about giving publicity in your area to the opportunities available in your training center. Release the teacher consultant on occasional Sundays to assist in other church schools, as invited. Offer opportunity in your own and nearby churches to send a limited number of their beginning teachers for 'apprentice' training under the teacher consultant." [4]

It is evident that such a scheme has splendid possibilities for practical leadership education in the local church. It combines learning by doing with expert supervision and careful planning. The Director of Leadership Education for the Presbyterian Church in the United States reports widespread interest in the plan, with the establishment of training centers throughout the entire constituency of the denomination.

The Volunteer Principle

There are those who maintain that dependence upon volunteers for religious instruction will ultimately end in failure. But for centuries the gospel of the evangelical churches has been in large measure transmitted by those who have made the teaching of religion an avocation. Humble folk, with little technical training, have been asked to undertake this task as a response to the unmerited grace of God. Men and women of great prominence have also given freely of their spare time that the cause of Christian education might go forward.

From the human viewpoint, it would be nice to turn our children over to a well-trained teaching order — people who know all the tricks of the trade. But after all, the example of the Master encourages us to believe that plain people can also understand, live, and teach his gospel. He did not draw on the professional religious classes for his leaders. Instead, he chose his disciples from the common people and gave them an incomparable course of leadership training. Protestantism must recover its faith in the potential service of the consecrated layman.

This is not to disparage the value of professional leadership in the free churches — splendidly trained ministers, musicians, and directors of religious education. However, it is not the function of the professional leader to supplant the volunteer worker. Rather, his success is to be judged by how many times he multiplies himself in the enlistment and training of nonprofessional leaders.

There are cogent reasons for taking this position. To turn the entire work of the Church over to a paid ecclesiastical group is to invite the triumph of formalism, mere ritual and tradition. We do well to remember that the Jews were priest-ridden in Jesus' day. The tragic fate of the Greek Orthodox Church in Russia is a more vivid reminder. Perpetuation of a free religion depends upon a sense of obligation on the part of lay folk not only to support the church financially but to take a hand in its control and its educational program. Many of the " new ideas " that have put life into Christian teaching have been advanced by laymen. The Sunday school itself is an outstanding example. An informed and participating laity serves as a wholesome check against ecclesiastical abuses. " Power corrupts, and absolute power corrupts absolutely." Perhaps most important of all is the example of a freewill offering of the self — a life dedicated to the service of the Master without hope of reward. Who can estimate the worth of a faithful Christian teacher, Boy or Girl Scout leader, gladly striving to do God's will — sharing the " good news "?